Makoto Ueda is a professor of Japanese and comparative literature at Stanford University, and the author of four books, including *Zeami, Bashō, Yeats, Pound* and *Matsuo Bashō*. He received the Gerald Brady Memorial Award from the Haiku Society of America for his contribution to haiku poetry and criticism in English.

The West has become familiar with Japanese haiku predominantly through the works of classical masters such as Bashō, Buson, and Issa. If the leading haiku poets in modern Japan are unknown in the West, it is simply because translations of their works have not been available.

This anthology presents, in English translation, twenty haiku each from the work of twenty modern poets. The writers have been selected to exemplify the various trends that have dominated Japanese haiku in the last hundred years, but the individual haiku have been selected for literary merit: more than anything else this is intended to be a book of poetry.

In the introduction Professor Ueda traces the development of the verse form to the present. Brief biographies of the twenty poets are also provided.

Haiku, by its very nature, asks each reader to be a poet. Thus, for each haiku the poetic translation is accompanied by the original Japanese and a word-by-word translation into English, and the reader is invited to compose his own poem, to enter into that private relationship with the poem that haiku demands.

現代日本俳句

選 集

上田　真・編訳・解説

トロント大学出版部（トロント・バッファロ）刊行

Modern Japanese Haiku
An Anthology

University of Toronto Press Toronto and Buffalo

© University of Toronto Press 1976
Toronto and Buffalo
Printed in Japan

DESIGN Peter Dorn RCA, MGDC

Library of Congress Cataloging in Publication Data
Main entry under title:
Modern Japanese haiku.
English and Japanese.
Added t.p. in Japanese has title: Gendai Nihon haiku
senshū.
1. Haiku – Translations into English.   2. English
poetry – Translations from Japanese.   3. Haiku.
I. Ueda, Makoto, 1931–   II. Title: Gendai Nihon
haiku senshū.
PL782.E3M6   895.6′1′508   74-75035
ISBN 0-8020-2147-6
ISBN 0-8020-6245-8 pbk.

100695

'76-05904

When we think of Japanese haiku, we usually think of the works of the old masters like Bashō, Buson, and Issa, paying little attention to the modern haiku poets, even though verse writing in the seventeen-syllable form remains as popular as ever in Japan today. Haiku lovers who do not read Japanese, in particular, are severely handicapped, as there has been only a small number of translations of contemporary Japanese haiku, in sharp contrast to Bashō's poems, some of which have been translated ten or fifteen times over. Many of the leading haiku poets of modern Japan still remain obscure in the West; some of them have not had a single haiku translated into a western language.

This book is intended to help narrow the gap. It presents, in English translation, samples from the works of twenty modern Japanese poets writing in the haiku form. The poets selected exemplify various trends that have dominated the history of Japanese haiku in the last hundred years, and in that sense they may be called representative haiku poets of modern Japan. In choosing the twenty samples from each of these poets, however, the criterion has been literary merit rather than historical significance, because more than anything else this collection is intended to be a book of poetry. It is only for the sake of convenience that the poets and their works are arranged in roughly chronological order. Each haiku has to be read as an independent entity.

Any poem demands a measure of active participation on the part of the reader, but this is especially true of haiku. With only slight exaggeration it might be said that the haiku poet completes only one half of his poem, leaving the other half to be supplied in the reader's imagination. The act of translating haiku therefore has negative implications, as it brings an extra person into what should be a private relationship between the reader and the poem. It is for this reason that the original Japanese wording, with a word-by-word English translation, is given at the bottom of the page for each haiku (the format follows the example set by Harold G. Henderson in his excellent *Introduction to Haiku* (Garden City, NY: Doubleday 1958), with which many readers of this book must be familiar). Brief notes on Japanese particles frequently used in haiku are also appended at the end of the book. Each reader is invited to read the original Japanese poem, or the word-by-word translation into English, and to compose a translation in his own style, or in the style of an English poet whom he considers appropriate. The translation given in this book should be considered *a* translation, showing one of the multiple meanings the haiku is capable of yielding when it is activated in the reader's mind.

In drafting my translations I received help from a number of people, to whom my sincere thanks are due. I am indebted, first of all, to various Japanese scholars who wrote explications on the poems collected in this anthology; even though I may not have followed their interpretations strictly, I found their comments most helpful. From a long list of those commentators I should at least mention the following names and express my gratitude: Abe Kimio, Hirahata Seitō, Kanda Hideo, Kusumoto Kenkichi, Matsui Toshihiko, Miyoshi Tatsuji, Nakajima Takeo, Ōno Rinka, Yamamoto Kenkichi, and Yoshida Seiichi (throughout this book Japanese names are given in the Japanese order, the surname appearing before the personal name or the name used in writing haiku). Mrs Elizabeth Wong kindly read the manuscript and offered many valuable suggestions. I am also grateful to the two readers provided by University of Toronto Press; their perceptive remarks on my manuscript were very helpful in the final stage of its preparation.

Last but not least, I wish to thank Mr Kaneko Tōta for looking over my draft translation of his poems and offering me the kind of advice that could be given only by the original author. While his kind comments gave me great encouragement, they also made me realize once again how nearly impossible it is to render a Japanese haiku into English without distorting or diluting (if not altogether losing) its original impact. To him and to all the other poets represented in this anthology I offer my humble apology for whatever unfavourable effect their poems may have suffered as a result of my translation.

M.U.
Los Altos, California

Modern Japanese Haiku

One day in December 1887 a young student registered at a small dormitory in a quiet residential district of Tokyo. He was pale, lean, and fragile-looking, but his fellow students soon found out he was an extraordinarily dynamic person. He was impassioned and eloquent when he talked. His topics were numerous, ranging from philosophy and politics to vaudeville and baseball; yet he was especially ardent when he talked about haiku. Indeed he seemed almost furious whenever the argument touched upon the degradation of contemporary haiku; he was afraid that the time-honoured seventeen-syllable poem might soon be dead and forgotten if it were to be left as it was. A practician as well as a theorist in all matters, he wrote haiku himself and persuaded others to do the same. Not satisfied with the small audience he had at the dormitory, he wrote articles for a Tokyo newspaper called *Nippon* as well. Favourable response came slowly but steadily from those who heard him talk or who read his writings. In his small untidy room at the dormitory there were always a few people discussing haiku with him. Before long he found himself the leader of a group that was determined to modernize haiku.

The student's name was Masaoka Noboru. He adopted the pseudonym Shiki in 1889, when he suffered a haemorrhage of the lungs. The pseudonym meant 'cuckoo,' a bird believed to continue singing even while spitting blood. Sadly, it turned out to be an appropriate name for him.

He never recovered from tuberculosis; after a prolonged period in which he was confined to bed, he died in 1902, at the age of thirty-five. Happily, however, the movement toward the modernization of haiku was well on its way by then. He had successfully brought about a poetic reform.

Haiku before the reform

Haiku as a verse form was more than three hundred years old when Shiki attempted to reform it. Its origin went back to *haikai*, a witty light-hearted variety of linked verse that became popular in the sixteenth century. Usually consisting of 36, 50, or 100 verses, haikai was composed by a team of poets jointly working under certain prescribed rules. The team leader would start off with an opening verse, called a *hokku*, in three lines of five, seven, and five syllables. Then the second poet would add the second verse, a couplet with seven syllables in each line. Subsequently these and other poets on the team would keep adding verses, written alternately in 5-7-5 and 7-7 syllables, until the poem reached the appropriate length. Matsuo Bashō (1644–94), famous for his haiku today, was also a superb haikai poet, and his creative genius helped a great deal in transforming haikai from a group game to an artistically mature poetic form, a form capable of expressing deep and complex human feelings.

Of all the verses constituting a haikai poem, the hokku was obviously the most important as it set the tone for the rest of the poem. That was why the most respected member of the team was usually invited to write it. The hokku also differed from other verses in that it was more independent. It could be appreciated all by itself, while the second, third, and all subsequent verses had to be seen as part of a longer poem. Bashō, in his travel sketches, often quoted hokku alone, omitting all the verses that followed. Later poets had occasion to write hokku alone, with little expectation that more verses be added. The practice cleared the way for the birth of haiku – completely independent hokku.

In the haikai tradition a hokku had to satisfy two main conditions. First, it had to contain roughly seventeen syllables, in the 5-7-5 pattern. Secondly, it had to include what was known as a 'season word,' a word suggestive of the season for which the poem was written. This second stipulation was a result of the haikai poets' wish to begin their joint poem on a realistic note. They knew they would be drifting to and fro on a balloon of fantasy throughout the verse-writing game, and

for that reason they wanted to have at least one slender rope that tied the balloon to the ground. It must be noted, however, that the major poets took liberties with these rules. Bashō, for instance, wrote a number of poems with more than seventeen syllables; some, indeed, had more than twenty syllables. Some of his hokku, including the famous deathbed poem, were also without a season word. Of course Bashō knew the rules, but he did not allow himself to be restricted by them.

The poets of the nineteenth century were not only restricted by the rules, but also wanted to increase the number of these restrictive rules. This was in a way a necessity under the circumstances, because the number of people who wrote hokku as a pastime had greatly increased, and these amateurs liked to have sophisticated rules to play what they considered an urbane game. With only a few rules the game would not have been interesting. The professionals, who taught verse writing for fees, readily invented many rules, thereby limiting the range of poetic themes, materials, vocabulary, and imagery. They set up different 'schools' of poetry, each school insisting that its rules were the most authoritative. The prime fault of all the schools, however, was that they failed to teach their students that the rules were, after all, designed only to aid in the writing of good poetry. They taught rules as if they were legal stipulations. The teachers themselves lacked the passion to write good poetry. Though they liked to link themselves with past masters, especially with Bashō, they had neither the expansive imaginative power nor the rigorous discipline of mind required of a true poet. Consequently the haikai and hokku written in the nineteenth century were, by and large, lifeless. The only exception was the work of Kobayashi Issa (1763–1827), but he was an obscure poet with no influence over the contemporary poetic scene. The poems that reached the reading public in the nineteenth century were trite, pretentious, and devoid of emotional appeal.

The birth of modern haiku

It was against this background that Shiki and his followers revolted. They wanted to bring about a poetic revolution that would shatter the stagnant state of affairs. Their manifestoes were most clearly stated in an article Shiki wrote for *Nippon* in 1896. With the lucidity characteristic of him he itemized the points of difference between his group ('we') and the other, more usual haiku writers ('they') of the day:

 1 We strive to appeal directly to emotion. They often strive to appeal to knowledge.

 2 We abhor trite motifs. They do not abhor trite motifs as much as we do. Between a trite and a fresh motif, they lean toward the former.

 3 We abhor wordiness. They do not abhor wordiness as much as we do. Between a diffuse and a concise style, they lean toward the former.

 4 We do not mind using the vocabulary of ancient court poetry or of modern vernacular slang, or words loaned from Chinese and western languages, as long as the words harmonize with the tone of the haiku. They rebuff words of western origin, confine the use of Chinese words within the narrow limits of contemporary convention, and accept only a small number of words from ancient court poetry.

 5 We do not attach ourselves to any lineage of classical haiku masters or to any school of contemporary haiku poets. They associate themselves with lineages and schools, and are smugly confident that they are especially honoured poets because of those associations. Accordingly they show an unwarranted respect for the founders and fellow poets of their own schools, whose works they consider unparalleled in literary value. As far as we are concerned, we respect a haiku poet solely for the merit of his poems. Even among the works of a poet we respect, we distinguish between masterpieces and failures. To define our position more precisely, we respect not the poet but the poem.

It is clear that Shiki was opposed above all to the mannerism of contemporary haiku. In his view the Japanese haiku of the nineteenth century were trite in motif, diffuse in style, pedantic in expression, restrictive in vocabulary, and too conscious of poetic factions. He sought the opposite of all those qualities in modern haiku, the haiku after his revolution.

The revolution, however, was not to come about easily. For one thing, the contemporary haiku masters stubbornly resisted it, as they wanted to maintain the secure position they currently held in society. Over the years they had done a number of things to enhance their social status. To bring authority to haiku and to themselves, they gave extravagant praise to past haiku masters, especially to Bashō. They built monuments and shrines to Bashō, virtually placing him alongside the Shinto gods and Buddhist sages. They tried to make use of government authority too. In 1873, for instance, they had some of their colleagues appointed as National Preceptors, a rank normally allotted to Shinto and Buddhist priests. To protect their interests haiku masters had built strong fortifications indeed.

In order to penetrate the fortress young Shiki had to resort to drastic means. He began his campaign by attacking not only certain influential poets of the day but their sacred idol, Bashō. Shiki was not blind to the virtues of Bashō's haiku, but he thought that they were limited in scope and that their virtues were outnumbered by their weaknesses. In his opinion Bashō's poetry was too passive in its implied attitude toward life and too biased against the bright colourful beauty of nature; timid and afraid of letting his imagination soar, the seventeenth-century poet always stayed within the realm of his actual experience. Bashō's verse also seemed lacking in complexity: he shied away from writing haiku on human life, which is complex, and preferred to compose poems on nature, which is simpler. In short, Shiki argued that Bashō's work was devoid of those qualities that form the crux of modern poetry – complexity, dynamic passion, soaring imagination. To seek a model in Bashō, he said, would be to go back to a pre-modern ideal – to allow a regression in poetry.

The poet whom Shiki introduced as a model for modern haiku writers was Buson. In his view Buson's haiku had practically everything that Bashō's did not have or did not have enough of. Buson's poetry was colourful, magnificent, and exquisite; it was fanciful, exotic, and startling. It was complex and yet concise, in some instances almost condensing a short story into seventeen syllables. Its scope was broad: it took its material not only from the poet's own life but also from the lives of others – priests, court ladies, common girls, merchants, travelling actors. It was objective and picturesque; by presenting objects or scenes that excited emotion, it avoided describing the poet's emotion itself. Buson's vocabulary was rich: it included words freely taken from contemporary slang, from court poetry, and from Chinese. Indeed Buson's poetry seemed to have all the ingredients which Shiki and his group sought in modern haiku. Shiki once went so far as to infer that seven or eight out of every ten haiku by Buson were excellent, while seven or eight out of every ten haiku by Bashō were mediocre. No doubt this was an exaggerated statement, but it shows how desperate Shiki and his fellow reformers felt when they faced the strong fortress of Bashō idolatry set up by contemporary haiku masters.

The other major task Shiki had to undertake was to do away with didacticism in haiku, thereby debunking the authority of the National Preceptors. This he did by persistently advocating the elimination of all extra-artistic elements from haiku. He said: 'Haiku is part of Literature. Literature is part of Art. Hence beauty is the ultimate value of Literature. The ultimate value of Literature is also the ultimate value of haiku.' The foremost concern of the poet, then, is to seek beauty, and not virtue, in nature or in human life, and to reproduce it faithfully in his haiku. Shiki saw more beauty in nature than in human life, and stressed the importance of realism in that connection. 'A haiku writer cannot do a more fitting thing,' he said, 'than encounter beautiful scenes of nature and copy them realistically.' As for the beauty in human life, Shiki advocated selective realism, for he took a man's life to be a mixture of the beautiful and the ugly. 'The haiku poet's task,' he observed, 'is to arrange in an orderly way the beautiful things that have existed in disorder, to match in an harmonious way the jewels that have been mismatched. When he writes a haiku on an actual scene, the poet should discard its ugly parts and pick up only its beautiful parts.' From our point of view today this concept of Shiki's is not striking; it is, indeed, rather simplistic and naive. But it should be remembered that Shiki was writing in Japan in the nineteenth century, and about a poetic form that had centuries of tradition behind it.

Shiki's insistence on purging all extra-artistic elements from haiku composition led to another important development that distinguished the new haiku from the old. This was the complete independence of a haiku as a poem. In his time the haikai was still alive, and poets often wrote a haiku as a hokku – that is to say, they wrote it as a verse that *could* be followed by other verses. As Shiki saw it, this fact threatened the autonomy of the poem and the identity of the poet. So he made a declaration that shocked his contemporaries: 'Hokku, written by a single poet, is Literature. Haikai, composed by a group of poets, is not Literature.' In order to distinguish an autonomous 5-7-5 syllable poem from the old hokku, Shiki proposed to employ the term haiku. The term had been in existence before his time, but had seldom been used. Now, revitalized by his new concept, the word came to circulate as widely as the concept.

All in all, then, a modern haiku conceived by Shiki could be described as follows. It is a poem written in roughly seventeen syllables and with a season word, as in former days. But otherwise it is entirely free of traditional rules, or of what the nineteenth-century masters had taught as unbreakable rules of composition. The poem is answerable only for the way in which the poet, as a free individual, sees beauty in nature or in human life. The poet has complete freedom both in the way in which he sees beauty and in the way in which he expresses it in his poem. The poem, therefore, can show any one of many types of beauty, colourful or austere, simple or complex. The merit of the poem lies in its individuality, in its independence, in its degree of freedom from stereotypes. A good poem will always be new in its motif, unhackneyed in its material, uninhibited in its vocabulary, and therefore direct in its emotional appeal and fresh in its overall impression. That is the *haiku*, as different from the *hokku* of old.

The radicals and the free verse movement

Shiki's untimely death in 1902 dealt no severe blow to the haiku reform movement. For one thing the movement had already gained wide support. The haiku pages in the newspaper *Nippon*, of which Shiki had been the editor, were attracting an increasing number of contributors. His haiku group had founded a magazine called *Cuckoo*, and it too was gaining in prestige. More important, Shiki had a number of talented and eager disciples who vigorously carried on the movement after their leader died.

Of all Shiki's disciples, two stood out above the rest: Kawahigashi Hekigodō and Takahama Kyoshi. Of the two, Hekigodō was the more zealous and agressive, and the movement's new leadership naturally fell on his shoulders. He succeeded Shiki as the editor of the haiku pages in *Nippon*, thereby establishing himself as one of the most influential haiku critics in the country. His position was solidified even more when his rival Kyoshi turned his creative energy to the writing of novels and essays. In 1903 Kyoshi himself conceded that Hekigodō was the most exemplary poet of the day.

Hekigodō's chief contribution to modern haiku was that he extended, or tried to extend, the borders of haiku far beyond what had been thought possible or legitimate. He was a tireless experimenter, and restlessly went from one experiment to another throughout his career. Of all his experiments the two most controversial were those on 'haiku without a centre of interest' and on haiku in *vers libre*. The idea of 'haiku without a centre of interest,' which he began to advocate in 1910, was based on his belief that a poem should come as close as possible to its subject matter, which is part of life or nature. He thought that if the poet tried to create a centre of interest in his poem he would inevitably have to distort his subject matter for the sake of that interest. 'To do away with a centre of interest and to discard the process of poetizing reality would help the poet to approach things and phenomena in nature as close as he can, without being sidetracked by man-made rules,' insisted Hekigodō.

It was a logical step, then, for Hekigodō to join some of his own students in experimentation in free verse, for obviously the 5-7-5 syllable pattern was a 'man-made rule.' Explaining his group's stand, he wrote in 1917: 'Any arbitrary attempt to mould a poem into the 5-7-5 syllable pattern would damage the freshness of impression and kill the vitality of language. We sought to be direct in expression, since we valued our fresh impressions and wanted our language to be vital. This soon led us to destroy the fixed verse form and to gain utmost freedom of expression.' Here, then, Hekigodō was extending Shiki's individualist doctrine to an extreme. Shiki had attempted to discard all the traditional strictures on the poet's individual talent, but had retained the 5-7-5 syllable pattern and the season word. But his successor saw the syllable pattern itself as restrictive and went on to discard it too. As for the value of the season word, Hekigodō's attitude was by and large affirmative. He defended the use of the season word in haiku by saying that every existence in the universe was integrated with the change of the seasons; in his opinion every poetic sentiment was imbedded in a season of the year. His idea of a new haiku, then, was a short *vers libre* usually with a season word.

Some of Hekigodō's students, led by Ogiwara Seisensui, went further in this direction. They rejected not only the seventeen-syllable form but the use of the season word as well. Seisensui, who had been writing in free verse before his teacher, later broke with Hekigodō on that account. In 1913, for instance, he remarked: 'The season word is a fetter fastened on the living flesh.' He also differed from Hekigodō in that he approached free verse from a symbolist's, and not from a naturalist's, point of view. 'A haiku begins with impressions and leans toward symbolism. It is a symbolist poem,' he said. 'To phrase it differently, a haiku emerges when a symbolic mood crystallizes into an expression – when an impressionistic perception takes a poetic form through the process of symbolic purification.' While Hekigodō wanted to catch the essence of his subject matter within itself and to express it in a rhythm unique to that subject matter, Seisensui tried to get a sensory perception of his subject matter within himself and to express it in a rhythm unique to that perception. In brief, he stressed the role of the man who perceives rather than the role of the object which is perceived; he valued the private, mystic vision of the poet. As a consequence his haiku became more and more mystical, more and more unconcerned with communication, as were the non-haiku poems of many Japanese and western symbolists in general.

Ozaki Hōsai, a student of Seisensui's, sought maximum liberation not only in the writing of haiku but also in life style. His pseudonym, Hōsai, imparts a strong sense of abandonment and release. At the age of thirty-eight he gave up all his possessions, leaving his lovely wife and resigning from his comfortable position as a branch manager of an insurance company. In search of a life of complete spiritual liberation, he served as an acolyte-handyman at one temple after another, barely supporting himself by doing chores around the temple buildings. Most of his finer haiku, which were written in those last years of his life, reflect the kind of simple, meditative life he was leading. Characteristically they are devoid of all decorative words, as his actual life was devoid of all superfluous activities. While most of the radicals wrote free-style haiku because of their poetic principle, Hōsai wrote it as a natural outcome of his spiritual life. His poetry is free, or represents an attempt to be free, not only in its verbal form but also in its moral implications.

The return to conservatism

The new direction the modern Japanese haiku was taking under the leadership of Hekigodō and Seisensui alarmed many poets of the day who were temperamentally less radical and experimental. Among the most alarmed was Kyoshi, who had been concentrating on writing novels and essays. More than ever before he must have felt guilty about contributing so little to the development of modern haiku, for he had by then taken over the editorship of the magazine *Cuckoo* but had suspended publication of haiku in it. He was also becoming somewhat weary of writing in prose. Thus in about 1912 Kyoshi made up his mind to try to re-establish himself as a haiku writer. First, he re-instituted haiku pages in the *Cuckoo*, himself assuming the position of haiku selector. He resumed writing haiku too, and began publishing them in the same magazine. He also wrote a number of essays on the art of haiku and published them in the *Cuckoo*, or in book form, or in both. Through all these activities he firmly took a conservative stand, vigorously defending the 5-7-5 syllable pattern and the use of season words in haiku.

Kyoshi's defence of traditional haiku was built on the theory that haiku is a classical form of poetry. In his view anyone who chooses to write in the haiku form has chosen to put himself against the background of the classical haiku poets and their works. 'Haiku is a type of literature in which form is a pre-determined factor,' Kyoshi observed. 'Its life depends on its classical flavour. With its seventeen-syllable form and its sense of the season, haiku occupies a unique place in the realm of poetry.' He had no objection, he said, to a poem written in *vers libre* or without a season word; he objected, however, if that poem was called a haiku. He insisted that anyone writing in a traditional verse form should observe the traditional rules that go with it.

As a logical extension of that argument Kyoshi later came to believe that haiku, with its traditional form and rules, presupposed a certain specific attitude toward life on the part of the poet. Haiku poets, he thought, look at life with 'a detachment of mind,' which makes it possible for them to bear with, or even enjoy, sad moments of life. In his view they would not get deeply involved with social and moral problems, as novelists and playwrights do. 'Haiku poets deal with an event in life in the same manner as they would deal with bush warblers and plum blossoms,' he said. 'They treat it shallowly but pleasurably, lightly but tastefully.' This was directly against the principles of naturalistic realism predominant in modern literature, as Kyoshi himself knew. He did not care, however, whether his theory and practice in haiku writing were behind the times, or whether some of his critics considered haiku a second-rate art form. He never wavered from his belief that haiku was, after all, a classical verse form and should be considered nothing more, and nothing less, than such.

Kyoshi's conservative position was, in theory, a drawback for modern Japanese haiku: at least in part, it proposed to bring haiku back to the point from which Shiki had started. But in reality Kyoshi's conservatist activities had the effect of making a large number of haiku writers regain confidence in the familiar 5-7-5 syllable form. As the editor of the *Cuckoo* he was a shrewd businessman and a tolerant, constructive critic as well. Contributors to the haiku pages increased year by year, and a number of new, gifted poets emerged. While Hekigodō died in frustration in 1937 and Seisensui carried on with a small group of comrades, Kyoshi gained an almost dictatorial power among an immense number of haiku-writing Japanese. Virtually all the major haiku poets who appeared after 1920 got their initial recognition through the help of Kyoshi as the editor of the *Cuckoo*. His poetry will yet have to stand the test of time, but his contribution as a critic and teacher is long past dispute.

Novelists as haiku poets

The *Cuckoo*, besides producing many fine poets, also introduced a talented novelist to Japanese readers. Natsume Sōseki, a friend of both Shiki and Kyoshi, had his first novel serialized in that magazine and immediately established himself as an imaginative new writer. Today his great fame as a novelist overshadows his haiku-writing activities, but in reality his career as a haiku poet was longer. He began writing haiku as a young man and became intensely interested in the form when young Shiki came to live in the same house with him for a time in 1895. In 1896 alone Sōseki wrote almost five hundred haiku. Most of these poems were sent to Shiki for critical comment. Sōseki's productivity declined after Shiki's death, and especially after his main creative energy turned to the writing of fiction. Yet he never stopped being a haiku poet. His early novels, such as *I Am a Cat* or *The Three-Cornered World*, show the sort of 'detachment of mind' characteristic of traditional haiku poets. And in his later years, when his naturalistic stand could no longer afford such a detachment, he wrote haiku in order to get moments of relief from the dark world of human strife which he was depicting as a novelist.

Another modern Japanese writer who wrote haiku throughout his career was Sōseki's protégé, Akutagawa Ryūnosuke. Akutagawa started to write haiku in earnest around 1916, the year when his short story 'The Nose' drew high praise from Sōseki and established him as a young literary genius. Two years later he came to know Kyoshi and asked for the master's expert advice from time to time thereafter. Akutagawa's haiku began to appear in the *Cuckoo,* and in no time they attracted the readers' attention with their novel imagery and polished style. By and large, however, he kept himself aloof from the contemporary trends of haiku. 'I am detached from both the radical and the conservative trend,' he used to say. He seemed more interested in the works of Bashō and his disciples; in fact, he took time out to write several stimulating essays on them. In particular his essays on Bashō became famous and exerted a measure of influence on the contemporary appraisal of that classical haiku writer.

The new traditionalists

In the meantime the *Cuckoo* was thriving. Kyoshi's broadly conservative stand attracted a number of talented poets, and he in turn used their works to display the high standards of his magazine. Between 1915 and 1917 he published a series of essays collectively called 'The Direction Which Future Haiku Should Take,' in which he singled out some of these newly emerging poets one after another and demonstrated what inspiring poems they had written. By 1920 the *Cuckoo* had become the leading haiku magazine in Japan. This success was due in no small measure to the fact that the works of these new poets, all of whom took the traditionalist position, were excellent by any standards and therefore had universal appeal.

Among the new poets the oldest and the most individual was Murakami Kijō. Living in a town some distance away from Tokyo, he had sent poems to the *Cuckoo* ever since its inception but had gained little recognition until 1917, when his *Collected Haiku* was published with Kyoshi's preface. Gathered together, his haiku revealed a powerful emotional appeal, since many of them embodied his deep, lifelong frustrations. He was deaf, and because of that had had to give up all his ambitions in his youth. He was poor, and had to struggle desperately to support his family of ten children. At one time his house was burnt down in a fire and he lost the few things he had owned. At another time he was dismissed from his job, and regained it only after his friends, who knew his reputation as a poet, intervened on his behalf. Thus Kijō's haiku are characterized by a sad but resigned acceptance of life's unfairness, by a half-hearted self-debasement and self-alienation, and by a deeply felt sympathy towards the weak and the crippled. They include a large number of poems on little animals and insects. It is not without reason that he is often compared to Issa.

If Kijō was the Issa among the new traditionalists, the 'modern Bashō' was Iida Dakotsu. Like Bashō, he loved nature and cherished a lonely life in the heart of it. While still in his early twenties he retired to a remote village near Mt Fuji and embarked on the life of a poet-recluse. He called himself Sanro ('mountain hut') and entitled his first volume of haiku *Collection of Poems at a Mountain Hut*. The best of his haiku collected therein show Bashō-like eyes that see nature in its naked, primitive charm. But, above all, Dakotsu resembled Bashō in that he imposed rigorous discipline on himself as a man and poet throughout his life. He was a man who hated compromises and petty manoeuvres; he wanted his life to be simple and straightforward, and was never afraid of facing its harshness. As a result his haiku came to have a wintry, austere type of beauty, as well as a quiet dignity, somewhat like the beauty of Bashō's later poetry. One critic has described the beauty of Dakotsu's haiku by comparing them to a huge moss-grown rock by a clear mountain stream.

Kawabata Bōsha was like Kijō in his affectionate interest in little animals and insects, and like Dakotsu in his rigorous

disciplining of the self, yet he created a poetic world uniquely his own. That world is generally known as the 'Bōsha Paradise,' because it seems to present a vision of Buddha's 'pure land' as conceived by Bōsha through intense spiritual contemplation of nature. A man who was ill for most of his adult life, Bōsha never tired of watching cats, butterflies, spiders and dewdrops; and, as he watched them closely, he sensed the workings of a super-human will that made them behave as they did. In the final analysis his poems are those of a Buddhist monk to whom this world is an imperfect image of the true world beyond, but who knows he can attain that other world only by means of this illusory world. Bōsha's poetry is the religious voice of the new traditionalist group.

Tomiyasu Fūsei, another member of the same group, chose to go in an entirely different direction in his pursuit of the poetic ideal. He wanted poetry to be more worldly, to be closer to the sphere of everyday life. He attributed this desire to his own personal temperament. 'In the end I always take a passive attitude toward every event that comes along my way,' he explained. 'Mine is a very weak sort of life, but it is also a type of life which has no sudden breakdown in mid-course.' Indeed he had a highly success-ful life both as a civil servant and as a haiku poet, basically because he always seemed to know how to accept things as they came. He never subscribed to the view that in order to be a better poet he should give up his high-ranking position in the government. In his opinion verse-writing was a diversion, a pastime that could and should be enjoyed by all peo-ple, regardless of what they did to earn their livelihood. His haiku may some-times seem too plain and relaxed, but they also have tenderness, lucidity, and a down-to-earth appeal, qualities that are becoming rare in modern poetry.

The flowering of modern haiku

As the years passed and as the conserva-tism of Kyoshi and the *Cuckoo* became immensely influential, there inevitably set in a reaction. As might be imagined, the revolt began within the *Cuckoo* group, where Kyoshi's authority was stiflingly powerful, and among young sensitive poets who abhorred the idea of being left behind the times. Their teacher, Kyoshi, was preaching as ever on the importance of plum blossoms and bush warblers as poetic subjects, but the world around them was going through a rapid change following World War I. Japan was be-coming westernized, and the Japanese life style was changing, too, after the western model. These young poets were worried, as Shiki had been a generation before, that haiku might become nothing more than a remnant of antiquated cul-ture. They did not deny the merit of the new traditionalists' works, but they were only too painfully aware that those poems did not reflect the spirit of the new age which was theirs.

The first poet to voice his dissatisfaction with Kyoshi's conservatism was Hino Sōjō, who had already had his haiku ac-cepted by the *Cuckoo* at the age of seven-teen. A youthful college student, he soon developed a distaste for the kind of tradi-tionalist attitude underlying the majority of poems published in that magazine. More than anything else he valued the free expansion of the poet's fancy. 'My guiding principle is not to be bound by principles,' he said at one time. 'In my opinion, faithfulness to a principle should give way to faithfulness to oneself,' he said at another time. He therefore ad-vocated venturing into areas of life hith-erto unexplored by haiku poets, especially the area of youthful, romantic love. What he advocated he put into practice: once he shocked his readers by writing a series of haiku depicting the first night of the bride and the groom after their wedding. He also wrote series of haiku on such topics as virginity, old bachelor girls, and nudist clubs – topics unthinkable in the previous haiku tradition. The *Cuckoo* group excommunicated him in 1936.

Looking back today, the merit of young Sōjō's poems seems by and large historical. Those poems helped to expand the realm of haiku in a direction no one else had thought of. As works of art they were in general not of exceptionally high quality, and his poetry became even more uninspiring as he grew older. Then, when he was forty-four, he was taken seriously ill and was bedridden until his death. Illness, poverty, and the memory of his past poetic fame constantly tormented him, and through this long period of suffering his poetry reached a new level of achievement. His later haiku had little of the shocking sensuality that characterized his earlier works. They were modest in attitude, calm in tone, and subdued in expression; they were, in short, close to the best of traditionalist haiku which he had once vehemently rejected.

Yet the revolt against the dominating conservative trend was carried on by other young poets, and with more satisfying results. The leader among them was Mizuhara Shūōshi, a young physician whose haiku had gained high acclaim through the pages of the *Cuckoo* in the early 1920s. Primarily a lyric poet, Shūōshi became increasingly dissatisfied with Kyoshi's conservative principles that seemed to restrict the poet's free emotional expression. Finally in 1931 he wrote an essay called 'Truth in Nature and Truth in Literature' and, making it his declaration of independence, left the *Cuckoo* group. A number of young poets who shared his views followed him. They already had their own haiku magazine, *Staggerbush*, and now they made it a place where they could freely pursue their own goals.

'Truth in Nature and Truth in Literature' was in essence an essay in praise of romanticism. At the start of the essay the author made clear the distinction between factual truth ('truth in nature') and imaginative truth ('truth in literature'). He then proceeded to charge that those *Cuckoo* poets who stressed the importance of 'detachment of mind' in the creative process were really trying to reach for factual truth. The traditionalists, Shūōshi thought, mistook the aim of science for the aim of literature, for literature has its *raison d'être* in being able to present imaginative truth. A poet should try to expand the borders of his imagination instead of limiting them; rather than imitating nature, he should be imitated by nature. Shūōshi concluded the essay with a cynical remark: 'If the whole aim of haiku writing were to grasp 'truth in nature,' the poet would need no assiduous study to gain new knowledge, no constant endeavour to enrich his mind. All he would have to do would be to roam about with a notebook in his pocket, following the shadow of a cloud.'

Shūōshi made a greater and more lasting impact on modern haiku than Sōjō. For one thing he wrote refreshingly beautiful poems to show what he theorized. In his first volume of haiku, published in 1930, he demonstrated that haiku is capable of embodying plenty of youthful lyricism. Haiku had never been lyrical before – not, at any rate, to the extent that Shūōshi's works were. His poems also had a bright, balmy beauty that had been lacking in traditional haiku. Shiki, indeed, had advocated that sort of poetry, but he seldom put it into practice successfully. And Shūōshi did all

this with no shocking language or imagery; his poetry always had quiet grace.

Another factor that helped Shūōshi in his successful revolt against the *Cuckoo* group was that he had the support of Yamaguchi Seishi, the most promising poet in the younger generation at the time. Seishi, too, had attained poetic recognition through the pages of the *Cuckoo*, but his poetry had shown such great individuality that Kyoshi, his initial patron, had predicted that he might abandon writing haiku altogether. Sure enough, Seishi stopped writing haiku along the traditionalist line. In 1935 he left Kyoshi and the *Cuckoo* group to join Shūōshi and the *Staggerbush* poets.

Seishi contributed to the development of modern haiku by exploring modernity in material and intellectuality in the creative process. 'The material should be new, and the sentiment should be deep,' he said in the postscript to one of his earliest collections of haiku. By new material he meant things that had lately become part of Japanese life in the industrial age, and his haiku included references to such things as smelting furnaces, revolvers, locomotives, elevaters. Young Sōjō had done this, indeed, but his sentiments were not 'deep' enough to touch on the innermost workings of the modern man's mind; his verses on the bride and the groom, for instance, were not quite free of old-fashioned sentimentalism about a wedding night. Seishi took a drier, more intellectual approach. He saw one's perception of truth as an essentially intellectual process; he also thought that the transformation of that perception into a seventeen-syllable form was basically intellectual. As a consequence, his characteristic poems have a hard cold surface behind which hides the sterile existence of modern man. No one before him had been so successful in bringing the wasteland of modern mechanized life into the realm of haiku.

By the late 1930s the new haiku movement initiated by Sōjō, Shūōshi, and Seishi had gained wide support among the haiku-writing populace, especially among urban intellectuals. The reason was obvious. Haiku was now modernized, far more completely than in Shiki's work. Or one might say that this new movement completed what Shiki had begun. Shiki had wanted to modernize haiku, but, as an invalid confined to bed, he did not live a modern man's life; he was not really a modern man. By contrast, Sōjō and Seishi were employees of

large commercial firms; Shūōshi was an obstetrician and operated a clinic, a hospital, and a school for midwives. All three lived in large cities which were growing even larger, and as young men they had experienced all the pain and suffering that were an inseparable part of modern urban life. They were, in short, forced to modernize haiku if they were to write haiku at all.

The rise of the humanists

The poets who remained with the *Cuckoo* were, of course, critical of the new haiku movement from the beginning. And soon they found an able spokesman in Nakamura Kusatao, who had begun writing haiku under Shūōshi but who had refused to leave the *Cuckoo* group. In the postscript to his first book of haiku, appropriately called *The Eldest Son*, Kusatao vigorously defended the traditionalist views. He stressed the importance of tradition by saying that one can attain self-knowledge only when one places oneself in the tradition of which one is a part. Through haiku writing he wanted, more than anything else, to see his essential being in proper historical perspective, and not from the viewpoint of the modern age alone. He voluntarily became 'the eldest son,' whose prime responsibility was to keep on nourishing the rich heritage handed down by his forefathers.

Holding such a view of haiku, Kusatao inevitably came to attach more importance to the moral perfection of the man than to the artistic perfection of the poem. In his opinion the poet should strive to improve his basic qualities as a man if he wants to write a good poem. This view would bring Kusatao closer to Shūōshi, who advocated the importance of learning and self-knowledge in verse writing, than to Kyoshi, who advised poets to observe nature with a detachment of mind. And indeed Kyoshi came to criticize Kusatao on this point, but the latter's stand remained unchanged. His belief, with its stress on the role of the man as against the role of the poet in verse writing, earned him the label of a 'humanist' haiku writer, distinguishing him from other traditionalist poets.

Kusatao did not remain isolated for long. Two of Shūōshi's followers, sharing the same sort of 'humanist' belief, soon came to join him. Ishida Hakyō, the younger of the two, had established himself as a youthful lyricist among the *Staggerbush* poets and had been considered the future leader of them all. But gradually he became dissatisfied with the kind of poetry written and advocated by Seishi; he did not like, above all, intellectualism. 'Haiku is not intellect,' he said. 'Rather, it is flesh. It is life.' He even went so far as to exclude haiku from literature. 'Haiku is not literature,' he declared. 'Haiku is raw life. . . . Composing haiku is synonymous with living life.' The sentences are terse, but what he means is sufficiently clear. He considered haiku part of a personal diary, and therefore he believed that an improvement in haiku writing presupposes an improvement in the haiku writer's moral being. The seriousness with which Hakyō wrote haiku was touching; it became the source of the powerful appeal in his later poems, many of which were the products of his long bedridden life.

The same type of seriousness, and with an even darker tone, lies in the poetry of Katō Shūson, the third of the 'humanist' trio. As a young boy he lost his father and had to spend his youth struggling to support his mother and brothers, since he was the eldest son. His poetry had no season of youthful lyricism; rather, it chose to probe deep into the agony of the human soul. Referring to the motive of his verse writing, he observed: 'As soon as we begin searching for truth and shake up our daily routine for that purpose, we discover an abysmal chasm lying under the surface at an unexpected spot. I wanted to bring back my personal discoveries from those chasms. I wanted to uncover my true self, the self that had been stirring silently beneath the peace and conventionalities of my daily life. And I wanted to fill my poetry with that experience, as if with a melancholy breath of air.' His first volume of haiku was fittingly called *Thunder in Midwinter*, and that became the title of a haiku magazine he founded too. Starting his literary career with a group of colourful lyricists led by Shūōshi, he steadily moved in an opposite direction and became the most sombre of the haiku writers of the day.

Kusatao, Hakyō, and Shūson were also called 'obscurists,' because some of their poems were extremely abtruse. This was because they wanted to be as faithful as possible to their innermost selves, even at the expense of their readers if necessary. They were not afraid of expressing chaos as chaos, or complexities as complexities, if they felt chaos or complexities in the inmost part of their hearts. They shunned intellectualization and denounced simplification. Always wanting to be true to themselves, they cared little about the popularity of their poems. Yet their admirers increased as years went by, and their influence became as widespread as that of any other major poet in recent times.

Haiku since World War II

World War II, with its inevitable restrictions on freedom of speech, put Japanese haiku writers in a difficult position. Along with other writers and artists, they were forced to support the government's wartime policies. The most they could do to show their disagreement was to declare, as some of them did, that they were primarily concerned with plum blossoms and bush warblers, and not with the war. Others chose to sing about the war, but with a detachment of mind that indicated neither agreement nor disagreement with the war policies. In any case haiku poets were overjoyed when the war ended in 1945. They could now express themselves more freely than ever before. Within a year's time more than three hundred haiku magazines sprang up all over Japan.

One of the most unique talents to blossom in the postwar period belonged to Saitō Sanki, though he had been recognized as a poet earlier. What distinguished him from other poets was that he was a spiritual foreigner; he did not feel spiritual affinity with traditional Japanese culture. In fact, before he became a poet, Sanki had been a dentist in Singapore and had dreamed of settling down somewhere in the Middle East for the rest of his life. Because of a change in the political climate he had to return to Japan in 1929, but he always remained an exile in his own country. When the war ended in defeat for Japan, he began to feel an affinity with his fellow countrymen for the first time. His poems, characterized by chilling nihilism and cynical humour, appealed to postwar Japanese readers, and his poetic fame rose. Sanki was a happy poet in Japan's unhappy years following the end of the war.

Another poet whose unique poetic talent became obvious in the postwar period was Tomizawa Kakio, though he, too, had been an established poet earlier. Unlike the 'humanist' poets, who valued life over art, Kakio insisted that the prime importance of a poem was its artistic perfection, arguing that the merit of a poem should not be based on the poet's sincerity. He thought that an attempt to evaluate the poet's integrity as revealed in the poem would ultimately lead the reader to an appraisal of the poet's life, which lies outside the poem. According to Kakio, a poem is autonomous and has its own world, a world distinctly different from this mundane society of ours. From this point of view he minimized the elements of daily life in his poetry and instead made abundant use of symbols far removed from the ordinary world. Inevitably his haiku became symbolic in the modern western sense. His poems expressed feelings of estrangement, melancholy, and ennui by means of surrealistic images. Though in a different way, some of his haiku became as obscure as those of the humanists in their implications.

A more typical postwar poet, Kaneko Tōta seemed to move in a direction opposite to Kakio at first. As a young poet he was deeply concerned with political and social problems, and his haiku treated such topics as atomic bombs, labour disputes, and American-Japanese relations. With him haiku became political and sociological to an extent it had never been before. But then he grew more and more interested in the formative elements of haiku. He began to argue that the most important thing for a poet was to reproduce his inner vision by his own rearrangement of forms taken from nature. In Tōta's view the poet is not a passive imitator who copies his subject as given by nature, but an active individual who creates his subject by wringing figures and images away from nature and by manipulating them in any way he sees fit. Here Tōta approached the theory of the avant-garde surrealistic artists; in fact, his poems have been called avant-garde haiku.

At this point one begins to wonder why poets like Kakio and Tōta chose to write in the haiku form. They might well have written symbolist or imagist poems in *vers libre*, as many other Japanese poets did. They must also answer Kyoshi's old charge that haiku is a classical form of poetry and that anyone who chooses to write in that form is obliged to accept its two main premises, the season word and the 5-7-5 syllable pattern. Their response would be that the season word is obsolete; today haiku does not have to have a season word because the seasons no longer play an essential role in Japanese life. They point out that buildings have air conditioning and central heating, that flowers can be bought at florists regardless of the season, and that birds, glowworms, and butterflies seldom come within the sight of urban dwellers, who are greatly increasing in number. As for the seventeen-syllable form, they want to retain it for their own reasons. Explaining why, Tōta says that he is attracted to the fixed verse form because it yields the beauty of finality in this life where nothing is final. A set form used by generations of people creates, he says, the feeling of familiarity, fulfilment, and ease for a modern man who is alienated, frustrated, and anxiety-ridden. According to Tōta, the 5-7-5 syllable pattern provides a poetic framework for a poet in the same way that an established religion provides a moral framework for a man.

From Shiki to Tōta the Japanese haiku has come a long way. If that century-long experience has proved anything, it has proved the vitality and adaptability of the haiku form. With the rapid westernization of Japan traditional forms of poetry have been exposed to the danger of extinction to a degree unknown in any previous age. Haiku has managed not only to survive the test, however, but to expand its borders vastly. Today it is thriving more than ever; there are hundreds of haiku magazines all over Japan. The variety of poetic styles is astounding too. On the one hand there are symbolist and surrealist haiku, and on the other there are traditionalist haiku emulating the style of Bashō; a beginning poet can select any style that lies between the two extremes and make it his own. Some critics have disliked such stylistic freedom and have argued that haiku has degraded itself in this century, that modern Japanese haiku is hopelessly corrupt. But if they say that, they will also have to say that modern Japanese culture as a whole is corrupt, for haiku has changed as Japanese life has changed. Japan today is a singular mixture of the East and the West; how to evaluate that fact depends upon one's idea of what a civilization should be. One thing is clear, however: whatever social and cultural changes Japan may go through in the years to come, haiku will survive. The history of haiku since Shiki's time bears testimony to that.

正 岡 子 規

Shiki was born on 17 September 1867 in a city called Matsuyama on the north-western coast of Shikoku. As a youth he wanted to be a statesman and moved to Tokyo, then a fast-growing city that seemed to offer him better educational and career opportunities. Indeed his life there turned out to be a very exciting and enriching one at first, but he over-worked and contracted tuberculosis in 1888. He left Tokyo University without graduating and became a reporter for the newspaper *Nippon* in 1892. When the Sino-Japanese war broke out two years later, he volunteered to be a war corre-spondent and travelled to China. As his friends had feared, he coughed blood during the journey and had to enter hospital on his return to Japan. He spent the rest of his life as a semi-invalid, his chief energy being exerted in the writing of haiku, tanka (traditional thirty-one-syllable poems), poetic diaries, and criti-cal essays. After attaining a measure of success in the haiku reform movement, he turned to tanka and initiated a similar reform in that verse form as well. As his health weakened, he entertained himself by painting watercolours. He died in Tokyo on 19 September 1902.

Hot spring in the mountains:
high above the naked bathers
the River of Heaven.

My younger sister
reads me an ancient war epic
this endless night.

山 の 温 泉 や 裸 の 上 の 天 の 川
Yama-no / yu / ya / hadaka / no-ue-no / ama-no-gawa
Mountain's | spa | : | naked-people | above | Heaven's-River
Ama-no-gawa *is the Milky Way which in China and Japan is imagined to be a river flowing across the sky. In a famous romance of the stars the Weaver Maiden (Vega) meets the Cowherd (Altair) across the river once a year.*

妹 に 軍 書 よ ま す る 夜 長 か な
Imōto / ni / gunsho / yomasuru / yonaga / kana
Younger-sister | by | war-epic | have-it-read | long-night | kana

Autumn chill:
with eyes glaring, there hangs
the mask of a demoness.

After the snake flees,
how quiet the forest is!
A lily flower.

秋 寒 し 眼 の 光 る 鬼 女 の 面
Aki / samushi / manako-no / hikaru / kijo-no / men
Autumn | is-cold | eyes' | glaring | demoness's | mask

蛇 逃 げ て 山 静 か な り 百 合 の 花
Hebi / nigete / yama / shizuka-nari / yuri-no / hana
Snake | fleeing | mountain | is-quiet | lily's | flower

Unceasingly
this stone on the summer moor
rests people.

New Year's Day:
dead chrysanthemums remain
at the garden's edge.

絶 え ず 人 い こ ふ 夏 野 の 石 一 つ
Taezu / hito / ikou / natsuno-no / ishi / hitotsu
Ceaselessly | people | rests | summer-moor's | stone | one

元 日 や 枯 菊 残 る 庭 の さ き
Ganjitsu / ya / karegiku / nokoru / niwa-no / saki
New-Year's-Day | : | dead-chrysanthemums | remain | garden's | edge

---

After killing
a spider how lonely I feel
in the cold of night!

I get down from my horse
and ask the name of the river—
an autumnal wind.

蜘 殺 す あ と の 淋 し き 夜 寒 か な
Kumo / korosu / ato-no / sabishiki / yosamu / kana
Spider | kill | after-that-time | lonely | night-cold | kana

馬 下 り て 川 の 名 問 へ ば 秋 の 風
Uma / orite / kawa-no / na / toeba / aki-no / kaze
Horse | descending | river's | name | when-ask | autumn's | wind

Shadows of the trees:
my shadow wavers with them
in the winter moonlight.

The wintry gust:
they have left a temple bell
by the roadside.

木 の 影 や 我 が 影 動 く 冬 の 月
Ki-no / kage / ya / waga / kage / ugoku / fuyu-no / tsuki
Trees' | shadows | : | my | shadow | moves | winter's | moon

凩 や 鐘 引 き す て て 道 の 端
Kogarashi / ya / kane / hikisutete / michi-no / hata
Wintry-gust | : | temple-bell | abandoning | road's | side

On a sandy beach
glassy chips sparkle
in the spring sunshine.

Blossoms have fallen
and the water is flowing
towards the south.

砂 浜 に き ら ら の 光 る 春 日 な か
Sunahama / ni / kirara-no / hikaru / haru / hinaka
Sand-beach | on | mica's | sparkling | spring | sunshine

花 散 つ て 水 は 南 へ 流 れ け り
Hana / chitte / mizu / wa / minami / e / nagare-keri
Blossoms | falling | water | as-for | south | to | flow-keri

My nurse,
awakening from a nap,
swats a fly.

A column of cloud—
onto my inkstone, an ant
has climbed.

看護婦やうたた寝さめて蠅を打つ
Kangofu / ya / utatane / samete / hae / o / utsu
Nurse | : | nap | awaking | fly | (acc.) | swats

雲の峰硯に蟻の上りけり
Kumo-no / mine / suzuri / ni / ari-no / nobori-keri
Cloud's | peak | inkstone | onto | ant's | climb-keri

The heart that loathes
this world thinks lovingly
of a thistle.

The snow melts:
bamboos uncoil themselves
where the sunlight falls.

世 を い と ふ 心 薊 を 愛 す か な
Yo / o / itou / kokoro / azami / o / aisu / kana
World | (acc.) | loathing | heart | thistle | (acc.) | loves | kana

雪 解 や 竹 は ね 返 る 日 の 表
Yukidoke / ya / take / hanekaeru / hi-no / omote
Snow-melt | : | bamboos | uncoil | sun's | front-side

A Buddhist monk
without waiting for the moonrise
takes his leave.

                                    For love and for hate
                                    I swat a fly and offer it
                                    to an ant.

ある 僧 の 月 を 待 た ず に 帰 り け り
Aru / sō-no / tsuki / o / matazu-ni / kaeri-keri
Certain | monk's | moon | (acc.) | without-waiting | return-keri

---

愛 憎 は 蝿 打 つ て 蟻 に 与 へ け り
Aizō / wa / hae / utte / ari / ni / atae-keri
Love-hate | as-for | fly | swatting | ant | to | give-keri

New Year's calendar:
in the month of May there is
a day for dying.

From the trellis
sponge gourds dangle down, each one
where it pleases.

初 暦 五 月 の 中 に 死 ぬ 日 あ り
Hatsugoyomi / gogatsu-no / naka / ni / shinu / hi / ari
New-Year's-calendar | May's | inside | in | for-dying | day | there-is

---

棚 の 糸 瓜 思 ふ 所 へ ぶ ら 下 る
Tana-no / hechima / omou / tokoro / e / burasagaru
Trellis's | sponge-gourds | wanting | place | to | dangle

夏 目 漱 石

Born in Tokyo on 5 January 1867, Sōseki received good training in the Chinese classics as a young boy, but specialized in English literature at Tokyo University and became a teacher of English after graduation. In 1900 he went to England as a government-sponsored scholar and studied in London for about two years. On his return home he was appointed Professor of English at Tokyo University. In 1905, solicited by his friend Kyoshi, he wrote a novel *I Am a Cat* for the *Cuckoo*; this marked the beginning of his illustrious career as a writer. All of his subsequent novels were accepted very favourably by the contemporary reading public. In 1907 he resigned his university post to devote his entire time to the writing of novels. Among his best-known works are *The Three-Cornered World* (1906), *The Wayfarer* (1912–13), *Kokoro* (1914), and *The Grass on the Wayside* (1915). Though he enjoyed great literary fame, his later life was not very happy, as it was hampered by attacks of stomach ulcer and neurosis. He died on 9 December 1916.

When a sparrow arrives
they move on the sliding screen,
shadows of the blossoms.

Onto a charcoal kiln
a vine keeps climbing, while
being burnt to death.

雀 来 て 障 子 に う ご く 花 の 影
Suzume / kite / shōji / ni / ugoku / hana-no / kage
Sparrow / coming / sliding-screen / on / moving / blossoms' / shadows

---

炭 竈 に 葛 這 ひ 上 る 枯 れ な が ら
Sumigama / ni / kazura / hai-agaru / kare-nagara
Charcoal-kiln / on / vine / crawls-up / while-dying

Is it showering?
A muddy cat is asleep
on a Buddhist sutra.

Against the autumn sky
a nameless mountain towers
higher than ever.

時 雨 る る や 泥 猫 眠 る 経 の 上
Shigururu / ya / doroneko / nemuru / kyō-no / ue
Showering | ? | muddy-cat | sleeps | sutra's | top

秋 の 空 名 も な き 山 の 愈 高 し
Aki-no / sora / na / mo / naki / yama-no / nao / takashi
Autumn's | sky | name | even | nonexistent | mountain's | more | is-high

The wintry gust:
it blows the evening sun down
into the ocean.

The crow has flown away:
swaying in the evening sun,
a leafless tree.

凩 や 海 に 夕 日 を 吹 き 落 す
Kogarashi / ya / umi / ni / yūhi / o / fuki-otosu
Wintry-gust | : | sea | into | evening-sun | (acc.) | blows-down

---

烏 飛 ん で 夕 日 に 動 く 冬 木 か な
Karasu / tonde / yūhi / ni / ugoku / fuyuki / kana
Crow | flying | evening-sun | in | moving | winter-tree | kana

---

On New Year's Day
I long to meet my parents
as they were before my birth.

Plum blossoms fall:
turning in the moonlit night,
a water wheel.

元 日 に 生 れ ぬ 先 の 親 恋 し
Ganjitsu / ni / umarenu / saki-no / oya / koishi
New-Year's-Day | on | not-born | prior | parents | long
A student of Zen Buddhism is sometimes asked to meditate on the origin of his life and, in so doing, tries to visualize his young parents prior to the time of his birth.

梅 ち る や 月 夜 に 廻 る 水 車
Ume / chiru / ya / tsukiyo / ni / mawaru / mizuguruma
Plum-blossoms | fall | : | moonlight-night | in | turning | waterwheel

A long day:
I take over his yawning
when he leaves.

It is quiet—
on the veranda, clippers
and peonies.

永 き 日 や 欠 伸 う つ し て 別 れ 行 く
Nagaki / hi / ya / akubi / utsushite / wakare-yuku
Long | day | : | yawn | passing-on | go-parting

寂 と し て 椽 に 鋏 と 牡 丹 哉
Jaku / to / shite / en / ni / hasami / to / botan / kana
Quietness | thus | doing | veranda | on | clippers | and | peonies | kana

---

Falling to the ground
it has trapped a gadfly,
a camellia flower.

Hazy moonlight night:
there must be love for
unlikely faces too.

落 ち ざ ま に 虻 を 伏 せ た る 椿 哉
Ochi-zama / ni / abu / o / fuse-taru / tsubaki / kana
Fall-instant / on / gadfly / (acc.) / have-trapped / camellia / kana

朧 夜 や 顔 に 似 合 ぬ 恋 も あ ら ん
Oboroyo / ya / kao / ni / niawanu / koi / mo / aran
Misty-moonlight-night / : / face / to / not-fitting / love / also / there-must-be

Into a man
as tiny as a violet
may I be reborn!

That inconspicuous
willow tree—of late it has
become green!

董 程 小 さ き 人 に 生 れ た し
Sumire / hodo / chiisaki / hito / ni / umare-tashi
Violet | to-the-extent-of | small | person | into | wish-to-be-born

---

有 耶 無 耶 の 柳 近 頃 緑 也
Uyamuya-no / yanagi / chikagoro / midori / nari
Inconspicuous | willow | lately | green | is

In the basin,
as I wash my face, there rises
autumn's shadow.

Not yet asleep,
a Buddhist monk sneezes:
midnight plum blossoms.

顔 洗 ふ 盥 に 立 つ や 秋 の 影
Kao / arau / tarai / ni / tatsu / ya / aki-no / kage
Face / washing / basin / on / rises / : / autumn's / shadow

眠 ら ざ る 僧 の 嚔 や 夜 半 の 梅
Nemurazaru / sō-no / kusame / ya / yowa-no / ume
Not-sleeping / monk's / sneeze / : / midnight's / plum-blossoms

The piercing cold—
I marry a plum blossom
in a dream.

It comes to my shoulder
longing for human company:
a red dragonfly.

寒 徹 骨 梅 を 娶 る と 夢 み け り
Kantekkotsu / ume / o / metoru / to / yumemi-keri
Bone-piercing-cold | plum | (acc.) | marry | thus | dream-keri

---

肩 に 来 て 人 な つ か し や 赤 蜻 蛉
Kata / ni / kite / hito / natsukashi / ya / aka-tonbo
Shoulder | to | coming | person | longs | : | red-dragonfly
Written shortly after recovering from a near-fatal illness in 1910.

I take my leave:
in my dream there stretches a streak—
the River of Heaven.

The grassy lawn:
amid the shimmering heat waves
a dog's dream.

別 る る や 夢 一 筋 の 天 の 川
Wakaruru / ya / yume / hitosuji-no / ama-no-gawa
Part | : | dream | one-streak's | Heaven's-River (Milky Way)

芝 草 や 陽 炎 ふ ひ ま を 犬 の 夢
Shibakusa / ya / kagerou / hima / o / inu-no / yume
Lawn-grass | : | heat-wave-shimmering | space-between | (acc.) | dog's | dream
Kagerou *refers to the heat waves seen on a warm, balmy spring day. In the Japanese poetic tradition these have been*
used as a metaphor for something evanescent, insubstantial, or unreal.

高 浜 虚 子

Born on 22 February 1874, in the district of Matsuyama where Shiki had lived as a young boy, and probably inspired by Shiki, Kyoshi was determined to become a man of letters early in life. Giving up formal education before entering college, he set up a publishing firm in Tokyo that specialized in haiku books. He was a good businessman and his firm prospered, especially after Sōseki's *I Am a Cat* appeared in his magazine *Cuckoo*. He also wrote novels, short stories, and essays, some of which enjoyed good public reception. From about 1913 on, however, his main interest was clearly in the seventeen-syllable poem, and before long he became the most influential haiku poet of his day. Amateur haiku writers from all over Japan looked up to him as their ultimate leader, and he frequently made trips to meet them and to give talks to them. A prolific poet, he wrote tens of thousands of poems in the 5-7-5 syllable form. In 1934 the *Complete Works of Kyoshi* were published in twelve volumes, but this edition soon became outdated as he vigorously carried on his creative activities. He was awarded the Order of Cultural Merits in 1954. He died on 8 April 1959 at the age of eighty-five.

The summer shower—
cutting straight through it, there goes
a white sailboat.

Through the back gate
of the house I am to rent
chrysanthemums are seen.

夕 立 を 真 横 に 走 る 白 帆 か な
Yūdachi / o / mayoko-ni / hashiru / shiraho / kana
Summer-shower | (acc.) | straight-through | runs | white-sail | kana

裏 戸 よ り 借 る べ き 家 の 菊 を 見 つ
Urado / yori / karu-beki / ie-no / kiku / o / mitsu
Back-door | from | to-rent | house's | chrysanthemums | (acc.) | have-seen

On distant hills
the rays of the sun fall ...
a withered moor.

A paulownia leaf
basking in the sunlight—
it's dropped to the ground!

遠 山 に 日 の あ た り た る 枯 野 か な
Tōyama / ni / hi-no / atari-taru / kareno / kana
Distant-hills | on | sun's | basking | withered-moor | kana

桐 一 葉 日 当 り な が ら 落 ち に け り
Kiri / hitoha / hi / atari-nagara / ochini-keri
*Paulownia | one-leaf | sun | while-basking | has-fallen-*keri

A gold bug—
I hurl it into the darkness
and feel the depth of night.

After the snake flees
the eyes that glared at me
remain in the grass.

金亀子擲つ闇の深さかな
Koganemushi / nageutsu / yami-no / fukasa / kana
Gold-bug | hurling | darkness's | depth | kana

蛇逃げて我を見し眼の草に残る
Hebi / nigete / ware / o / mishi / me-no / kusa / ni / nokoru
Snake | fleeing | me | (acc.) | having-looked | eyes' | grass | in | remain

---

The summer moon—
on the plate lies an apple
with its redness lost.

Under the autumnal
sky, a wild chrysanthemum
lacking a petal.

夏 の 月 皿 の 林 檎 の 紅 失 す
Natsu-no / tsuki / sara-no / ringo-no / kō / shissu
Summer's | moon | plate's | apple's | redness | loses

秋 天 の 下 に 野 菊 の 花 弁 欠 く
Shūten-no / shita / ni / nogiku-no / kaben / kaku
Autumn-sky's | underneath | in | wild-chrysanthemum's | petal | lacks

*The sun in the sky
is mirrored darkly on the water
where tadpoles live.*

*Over the children
picking herbs on the fields something
gigantic passes.*

天 日 の う つ り て 暗 し 蝌 蚪 の 水
Tenjitsu-no / utsurite / kurashi / kato-no / mizu
Heavenly-sun's | mirroring | is-dark | tadpoles' | water

草 を 摘 む 子 の 野 を 渡 る 巨 人 か な
Kusa / o / tsumu / ko-no / no / o / wataru / kyojin / kana
Grass | (acc.) | picking | children's | field | (acc.) | passing | giant | kana

---

It begins to bud—
close to the trunk of the great tree
I strain my ears to listen.

Floating away—
the turnip leaves—and how
swiftly they go!

芽 ぐ む な る 大 樹 の 幹 に 耳 を 寄 せ
Megumu / naru / taiju-no / miki / ni / mimi / o / yose
Budding | becomes | large-tree's | trunk | ears | (acc.) | bringing-close

流 れ 行 く 大 根 の 葉 の 早 さ か な
Nagare-yuku / daikon-no / ha-no / hayasa / kana
Floating-away | turnip's | leaves' | swiftness | kana

In an instant
it has become a flame: a spider
in the burning grass.

                                        A butterfly
                                        in the cold: it flies in pursuit
                                        of its own soul.

ばつと火になりたる蜘蛛や草を焼く
Patto / hi / ni / nari-taru / kumo / ya / kusa / o / yaku
Instantly | flame | to | has-become | spider | : | grass | (acc.) | burn

凍蝶の己が魂追うて飛ぶ
Itechō-no / onoga / tamashii / ōte / tobu
Freezing-butterfly's | self's | soul | pursuing | flies

I gaze at the river.
A banana peel I held
slips from my hand.

When I set
something down, there emerges
autumn's shadow.

川 を 見 る バ ナ ナ の 皮 は 手 よ り 落 ち
Kawa / o / miru / banana-no / kawa / wa / te / yori / ochi
River / (acc.) / look / banana's / peel / as-for / hand / from / falling

も の 置 け ば そ こ に 生 れ ぬ 秋 の 蔭
Mono / okeba / soko / ni / umarenu / aki-no / kage
Thing / when-put / that-place / in / has-been-born / autumn's / shadow

Midwinter's cold:
I go to visit a sick man
—he is already dead!

A dead chrysanthemum
and yet—isn't there still something
remaining in it?

大 寒 や 見 舞 に 行 け ば 死 ん で を り
Daikan / ya / mimai / ni / yukeba / shinde-ori
Great-cold | : | inquiry (after one's health) | for | when-go | has-been-dead

---

枯 菊 に 尚 ほ 或 物 を と ど め ず や
Karegiku / ni / nao / arumono / o / todomezu / ya
Dead-chrysanthemum | in | still | something | (acc.) | not-retain | ?

He says a word,
and I say a word—autumn
is deepening.

Last year and this year—
piercing through the two, something
like a pole.

彼 一 語 我 一 語 秋 深 み か も
Kare / ichigo / ware / ichigo / aki / fukami / kamo
He | one-word | I | one-word | autumn | deepening | kamo

去 年 今 年 貫 く 棒 の 如 き も の
Kozo / kotoshi / tsuranuku / bō-no / gotoki / mono
Last-year | this-year | piercing | pole's | resembling | thing
Written on New Year's Day, 1951.

河 東 碧 梧 桐

Hekigodō was born in Matsuyama on 26 February 1873. Since his father was a Confucian scholar, he was well tutored in the Chinese classics in his childhood. He became a classmate of Kyoshi's at middle school and remained close to him throughout his life. With Kyoshi he gave up school in 1894 and went to Tokyo, where he became a newspaper reporter. He was a man of many talents, however, and made a name as a literary scholar, noh dancer, art critic, calligrapher, social commentator, and mountain climber, besides being a writer and critic of haiku. He travelled a great deal and wrote many travel sketches; he visited Europe and North America in 1921, China and Mongolia in 1924. By and large he was too restless and too interested in experiment to stay at one project for long, and thus he never achieved as much as his abundant talents had appeared to promise for him. As he grew older he became more and more isolated from the mainstream of literary and cultural activities. He devoted more and more of his time to the study of classical haiku, especially of Buson. He died in Tokyo on 1 February 1937.

From a bathing tub
I throw water into the lake—
slight muddiness appears.

Wheat harvesting time—
a man who looks like a robber
passes by.

行水を捨てて湖水のささ浊り
Gyōzui / o / sutete / kosui-no / sasanigori
Bathing-water | (acc.) | throwing-away | lakewater's | slight-muddiness

麦の秋盗人らしき者通る
Mugi-no / aki / nusubito / rashiki / mono / tōru
Wheat's | harvest-time | robber | resembling | person | passes

Startled
I wake from a midday nap
all alone.

For a baby who
keeps crying she lights a lamp:
evening in autumn.

愕然として昼寝さめたる一人哉
Gakuzen / to / shite / hirune / same-taru / hitori / kana
Startle | thus | doing | midday-nap | wakened | one-person | kana

泣きやまぬ子に灯ともすや秋の暮
Naki / yamanu / ko / ni / hi / tomosu / ya / aki-no / kure
Crying | not-stopping | child | for | lamp | lights | : | autumn's | evening

Fallen off the eaves,
a pile of snow blocks the street
in a slum area.

A fasting man
craves for water at midnight:
a flash of lightning.

軒 落 ち し 雪 窮 巷 を 塞 ぎ け り
Noki / ochishi / yuki / kyūkō / o / fusagi-keri
Eaves / has-fallen / snow / slum / (acc.) / blocks-keri

断 食 の 水 恋 ふ 夜 半 や 稲 光
Danjiki-no / mizu / kou / yowa / ya / inabikari
Faster's / water / craving / midnight / : / lightning

After the riot
an incomparably beautiful
moonlit night.

Unexpectedly
a chick has hatched —
midwinter rose.

暴 動 の 後 に ま た な き 月 夜 か な
Bōdō-no / ato-ni / mata / naki / tsukiyo / kana
Riot's / after / another / non-existent / moonlight-night / kana

思 は ず も ヒ ョ コ 生 れ ぬ 冬 薔 薇
Omowazumo / hiyoko / umarenu / fuyu / sōbi
Unexpectedly / chick / has-been-born / winter / rose

The horse alone
has unexpectedly returned—
flitting fireflies ...

Clawing the void
lies the corpse of a crab:
mountains of cloud.

馬 ひ と り 忽 と 戻 り ぬ 飛 ぶ 螢
Uma / hitori / kotsu-to / modorinu / tobu / hotaru
Horse / alone / suddenly / has-returned / flying / fireflies

空 を は さ む 蟹 死 に を る や 雲 の 峰
Kū / o / hasamu / kani / shini / oru / ya / kumo-no / mine
Void / (acc.) / claws / crab / being-dead / lies / : / cloud's / peak
Kumo-no mine *refers to towering white comulus clouds, often seen against the clear blue sky on a hot summer day.*

In the faint light of dawn
a tree blossoming in white,
the field sprinkled with dew.

                              A sleeping cow?
                              A boulder? It could be either.
                              Grass sprouts out.

ほ の 明 け に 花 白 き 木 や 露 の 原
Honoake / ni / hana / shiroki / ki / ya / tsuyu-no / hara
Faint-dawn / at / blossoms / white / tree / : / dew's / field

寝 牛 と も 石 と も 見 え て 草 萌 る
Neushi / to / mo / ishi / to / mo / miete / kusa / moyuru
Sleeping-cow / thus / also / stone / thus / also / appearing / grass / sprouts

Wrestlers are aboard
the ferry; why has it become
stormy weather?

In the distance
a tall tree
near summertime
stands
above multitudinous roofs.

相 撲 乗 せ し 便 船 の な ど 時 化 と な り
Sumō / noseshi / binsen-no / nado / shike / to / nari
Wrestlers | aboard | ferry's | why | storm | thus | becoming
An example of 'haiku without a centre of interest' which was cited by Hekigodō himself.

遠 く 高 き 木 夏 近 き 立 て り 畳 む 屋 根 に
Tōku / takaki / ki / natsu / chikaki / tateri / tatamu / yane / ni
Far | tall | tree | summer | near | stands | manifold | roofs | on

---

Until I hit the fly
the fly-swatter
did not exist.

Mountain roses bloom:
factory girls
at the windows
of a tenement house.

蠅打つまで蠅叩きなかりし
Hae / utsu / made / hae-tataki / nakarishi
Fly | hit | until | fly-swatter | was-non-existent

山吹咲く工女が窓々の長屋
Yamabuki / saku / kōjo-ga / mado-mado-no / nagaya
Mountain-roses | bloom | factory-girls' | window-window's | tenement-house

---

Whitening with dawn,
the sliding screen:
on it a moth
high up.

Oyster stew
has become cold—
same old
wife of mine.

明白む障子の蛾高し
Ake / shiramu / shōji-no / ga / takashi
Dawning / whitens / sliding-screen's / moth / is-high

牡蠣飯冷えたりいつもの細君
Kaki-meshi / hie-tari / itsumo-no / saikun
Oyster-meal / has-become-cold / usual / wife

Father had known,
didn't say a word:
pampas grass in the garden.

I pull out a stalk of grass,
the root's whiteness
and depth—
I bear with the sight.

父 は わ か つ て ゐ た 黙 つ て ゐ た 庭 芒
Chichi / wa / wakatte / ita / damatte / ita / niwa / susuki
Father | as-for | aware | was | silent | was | garden | pampas-grass
Susuki *normally grows in the wilderness. In autumn its bushy, beige-coloured tufts create a lovely impression.*

草 を ぬ く 根 の 白 さ 深 さ に 堪 へ ぬ
Kusa / o / nuku / ne-no / shirosa / fukasa / ni / taenu
Grass | (acc.) | pull-out | root's | whiteness | depth | with | bear

---

荻 原 井 泉 水

Seisensui was born in Tokyo on 16 June 1884. A bright student, he published an essay on language reform at the age of fifteen. His interest in languages continued, and he specialized in linguistics at Tokyo University, graduating in 1908. His other interest was German literature, and he translated some of Goethe's works into Japanese. His training in linguistics and in western literature inevitably made him sceptical of the methodology of traditional haiku, which he had begun writing while in middle school. He readily joined Hekigodō in advocating 'haiku without a centre of interest.' In 1911 he founded a new haiku magazine, *Stratus*, which soon came to serve as the main outlet for radical free-style haiku. He himself began writing in free verse in 1914. In the early 1920s his wife, child, and mother died in rapid succession, and he lived a Buddhist pilgrim's life for a time. He eventually re-married, but a religious flavour remained in many of his poems thereafter. Beside free-style haiku he has written a great many essays and travel sketches; all told, his books number nearly four hundred. Today he lives in the seaside town at Kamakura.

Sunday fisherman!
Prison wall
mirrored in the water.

A morning
of babies crying,
of roosters crowing,
with all their might.

日曜 の 釣 人 よ 監獄 の 塀 が 映 る 水
Nichiyō-no / tsuribito / yo / kangoku-no / hei / ga / utsuru / mizu
Sunday's | fisherman | ! | prison's | wall | (nomin.) | reflected | water

力 一 ぱ い に 泣 く 児 と 啼 く 鶏 と の 朝
Chikara / ippai / ni / naku / ko / to / naku / niwatori / to / no / asa
Strength | full-capacity | at | crying | child | and | crowing | rooster | and | 's | morning

*Pedlar's
aged shadow
in the setting sun
stretches to its limit.*

*Awaiting the ball,
maidens' arms
form a grove
and sway.*

物 売 の 老 い し 影 夕 日 に 伸 び き り た り
Monouri-no / oishi / kage / yūhi / ni / nobikiri-tari
Pedlar's / aged / shadow / evening-sun / in / has-stretched-to-the-limit

毬 を 待 つ 少 女 等 が 手 は 林 な し て 戦 げ り
Mari / o / matsu / otomera-ga / te / wa / hayashi / nashite / soyogeri
Ball / (acc.) / awaiting / maidens' / arms / as-for / grove / making / sway

The load taken down,
a chilly horse!
It rains.

Dandelions,
dandelions
on the sandy shore—
spring
opens its eyes.

荷 が お ろ さ れ て 寒 い 馬 よ 雨 降 る
Ni / ga / orosarete / samui / uma / yo / ame / furu
Load / (nomin.) / taken-down / cold / horse / ! / rain / falls

た ん ぽ ぽ た ん ぽ ぽ 砂 浜 に 春 が 目 を 開 く
Tanpopo / tanpopo / sunahama / ni / haru / ga / me / o / aku
Dandelions / dandelions / sandy-shore / on / spring / (nomin.) / eyes / (acc.) / opens

As there is water
in the rice paddy,
the blue sky
is deeply ploughed.

In the sky
walk
serenely—
the moon alone.

水 あ れ ば 田 に 青 空 が 深 く 鋤 か れ あ る
Mizu / areba / ta / ni / aozora / ga / fukaku / sukare / aru
Water / as-is / rice-paddy / in / blue-sky / (nomin.) / deeply / ploughed / is

---

空 を あ ゆ む 朗 々 と 月 ひ と り
Sora / o / ayumu / rōrō-to / tsuki / hitori
Sky / (acc.) / walk / serenely / moon / alone
Ayumu can mean either '(I) walk' or '(the moon) walks.' No doubt the ambiguity is intentional.

In Buddha
I believe:
wheat-ears' green
truth.

Night is
ice-bag's
white silence—
you and I.

仏 を 信 ず 麦 の 穂 の 青 き し ん じ つ
Hotoke / o / shinzu / mugi-no / ho-no / aoki / shinjitsu
Buddha | (acc.) | believe | wheat's | ears' | green | truth

夜 が 氷 嚢 の 白 い 沈 黙 で お 前 と 私
Yoru / ga / hyōnō-no / shiroi / chinmoku / de / omae / to / watashi
Night | (nomin.) | ice-bag's | white | silence | being | you | and | me

In the fog
for a friend to come out of the fog
I keep waiting.

									Butterfly's wings,
									most beautiful in the world;
									ants
									pull them.

霧 に 霧 を い で て く る 友 を 待 ち て お る
Kiri / ni / kiri / o / idete / kuru / tomo / o / machite / oru
Fog / in / fog / (acc.) / leaving / comes / friend / (acc.) / awaiting / am

蝶 の 羽 世 に も う る わ し 蟻 ら こ れ を 曳 く
Chō-no / hane / yo / ni / mo / uruwashi / ari-ra / kore / o / hiku
Butterfly's / wings / world / in / even / is-beautiful / ants / these / (acc.) / pull

Flowers are there,
and yet,
looking for flowers,
a butterfly.

Stone's plumpness
turns into snow.

花 が あ る の に 花 を さ が し て い る 蝶 々
Hana / ga / aru / no-ni / hana / o / sagashite / iru / chōchō
Flowers | (nomin.) | there-are | yet | flowers | (acc.) | seeking | is | butterfly

---

石 の ま ろ さ 雪 に な る
Ishi-no / marosa / yuki / ni / naru
Stone's | plumpness | snow | to | turns

Peony:
one petal,
another petal,
moving,
opening,
puts itself in order.

A stone
and a stone
in the moonlit night
nestle against one another.

牡 丹 一 弁 一 弁 の 動 き つ つ 開 き つ つ 姿 と と の う
Botan / ichiben / ichiben-no / ugoki-tsutsu / hiraki-tsutsu / sugata / totonou
Peony | one-petal | one-petal | moving | opening | form | gets-in-shape

石 と 石 月 夜 寄 り そ う
Ishi / to / ishi / tsukiyo / yorisou
Stone | and | stone | moonlight-night | nestle

As the butterfly of my house,
it flies about
for a while.

From the cage
fireflies
one by one
turn into stars.

うちの蝶としてとんでいるしばらく
Uchi-no / chō / to-shite / tonde / iru / shibaraku
Home's | butterfly | as | flying | is | awhile

かごからほたる一つ一つを星にする
Kago / kara / hotaru / hitotsu / hitotsu / o / hoshi / ni / suru
Cage | from | fireflies | one | one | (acc.) | stars | into | make

Because the fence is there
my neighbour's camellia
falls
into my yard.

Hot day's
hollowness:
white butterfly
all alone
passes.

垣 が あ る の で 隣 の つ ば き う ち に お ち る
Kaki / ga / aru / no-de / tonari-no / tsubaki / uchi / ni / ochiru
Fence / (nomin.) / there-is / therefore / neighbour's / camellia / my-home / into / falls

暑 い 日 の 空 白、 白 い 蝶 一 羽 に て 通 る
Atsui / hi-no / kūhaku / shiroi / chō / ichiwa / nite / tōru
Hot / days' / hollowness / white / butterfly / one / with / passes

村 上 鬼 城

Kijō was born in Tokyo on 17 May 1865. As a youth he wanted to enter the civil service and studied law, but he had to give up the plan when he became deaf because of an illness. In 1894 he began working as a scribe at the courthouse in Takasaki, a rustic town about sixty miles northwest of Tokyo. His earnings were small, and he had a difficult time supporting his two sons and eight daughters. Even that source of income stopped in 1915 when he was dismissed from his job, but his friends intervened and regained it for him the following year. In 1927 his home was burnt down in a fire. Through all these unhappy years haiku writing provided a consolation for him. At first his poetry attracted little attention, but gradually it gained admirers. Kyoshi met Kijō in 1913 and gave him encouragement. In 1916 the *Cuckoo* published his essay on Sugiyama Sanpū, a classical haiku poet who had been, like him, deaf. The following year his first *Collected Haiku*, with a preface by Kyoshi, was published; he published two more collections of haiku in his lifetime. He died in Takasaki on 17 September 1938.

Crawling up and up
on a blade of summer grass
an abandoned silkworm.

First autumn morning:
the mirror I stare into
shows my father's face.

夏 草 を 這 ひ 上 り た る 捨 蚕 か な

Natsukusa / o / haiagari-taru / sutego / kana

Summer-grass | (acc.) | has-crawled-up | abandoned-silkworm | kana

Silkworms are raised at farmhouses; they do not live in the wilds. Sutego is a silkworm cast away by the farmer for one reason or another, usually because it is ailing.

今 朝 秋 や 見 入 る 鏡 に 親 の 顔

Kesa / aki / ya / miiru / kagami / ni / oya-no / kao

This-morning | autumn | : | stare | mirror | in | parent's | face

Balmy autumn day:
on a stone, biting it,
a red dragonfly.

The winter sun:
blocking the way ahead of me,
my own shadow.

小 春 日 や 石 を 嚙 み 居 る 赤 蜻 蛉
Koharubi / ya / ishi / o / kami / iru / akatonbo
Balmy-autumn-day | : | stone | (acc.) | biting | is | red-dragonfly

冬 の 日 や 前 に 塞 が る 己 が 影
Fuyu-no / ni / ya / mae / ni / fusagaru / ono-ga / kage
Winter's | sun | : | front | in | blocking | self's | shadow

Yearning towards
its own shadow, there creeps
a grub.

I long to go out,
yet I am fearful of people —
cold season lingers.

己 が 影 を 慕 ふ て 這 へ る 地 虫 か な
Ono-ga / kage / o / shitōte / haeru / jimushi / kana
Self's / shadow / (acc.) / yearning / crawls / grub / kana

世 を 恋 う て 人 を お そ る る 余 寒 か な
Yo / o / kōte / hito / o / osoruru / yokan / kana
World / (acc.) / loving / people / (acc.) / fear / lingering-cold / kana

---

Spring night:
sitting around a lamp, relax
blind men in a group.

Long rainy days:
a weed, cut at the root,
raises its head.

春 の 夜 や 灯 を 囲 み 居 る 盲 者 達
Haru-no / yo / ya / hi / o / kakomi / iru / mekura-tachi
Spring's | night | : | lamp | (acc.) | surrounding | are | blind-men

---

さ み だ れ や 起 き 上 が り た る 根 無 し 草
Samidare / ya / okiagari-taru / nenashi-gusa
June-rain | : | has-risen | rootless-grass

How white they are!
It darkens, no one trampling
the fallen blossoms.

Floating duckweed:
a spider passes over it —
the water, calm.

しらしらと人踏まで暮るる落花かな
Shira-shira / to / hito / fumade / kururu / rakka / kana
White-white | thus | person | without-trampling | darkens | fallen-flowers | kana

浮草や蜘蛛渡りゐて水平ら
Ukikusa / ya / kumo / watari-ite / mizu / taira
Duckweeds | : | spider | passing | water | calm

On the Buddha's
august face some pockmarks show:
autumnal rain.

The moment two bubbles
are united, they both vanish.
A lotus blooms.

御仏のお顔のしみや秋の雨
Mihotoke-no / okao-no / shimi / ya / aki-no / ame
Lord-Buddha's / august-face's / spots / : / autumn's / rain

水泡の相依れば消ゆ蓮の花
Suihō-no / aiyoreba / kiyu / hasu-no / hana
Water-bubbles' / when-approach-together / vanish / lotus's / flower

A winter hornet
without a place to die
staggers along.

A water spider
bounces on the water, and
the water is like steel.

冬 蜂 の 死 に ど こ ろ な く 歩 き け り
Fuyubachi-no / shinidokoro / naku / aruki-keri
Winter-hornet's | place-for-death | non-existent | walks-keri

---

水 す ま し 水 に 跳 て 水 鉄 の 如 し
Mizusumashi / mizu / ni / hanete / mizu / tetsu-no / gotoshi
Water-spider | water | on | bouncing | water | steel's | resembles

---

A winter stream:
abloom on a little stone,
blossoms of water.

Spring rain:
I am certain I saw
the spirits of stones.

冬 川 や 小 さ き 石 に 浪 の 花
Fuyu-kawa / ya / chiisaki / ishi / ni / nami-no / hana
Winter-stream | : | small | stone | on | waves' | blossoms

春 雨 や た し か に 見 た る 石 の 精
Harusame / ya / tashika / ni / mi-taru / ishi-no / sei
Spring-rain | : | certainty | with | have-seen | stones' | spirits

Cold day in spring:
bumping into this and that,
a blind dog walking.

Not able to bear
the stillness, a mud snail
has moved!

春寒 や ぶ つ か り 歩行 く 盲犬
Haru-samu / ya / butsukari / aruku / mekura-inu
Spring-cold | : | bumping | walks | blind-dog

静 か さ に 堪 へ で た に し の 移 り け り
Shizukasa / ni / taede / tanishi-no / utsuri-keri
Stillness | with | not-bearing | mud-snail's | moves-keri

Hot autumn day—
swarming to the grass seed,
a flock of sparrows.

Clutching a lump
of earth, it lies dying—
a grasshopper.

秋 暑 し 草 の 実 に つ く む ら 雀
Aki / atsushi / kusa-no / mi / ni / tsuku / murasuzume
Autumn | is-hot | grass's | seed | to | cling | flock-of-sparrows

土 く れ を か か へ て 死 ぬ る 蝗 か な
Tsuchikure / o / kakaete / shinuru / inago / kana
Earth-lump | (acc.) | clutching | dies | grasshopper | kana

A late autumn scene. A grasshopper is dying as all the crops have disappeared from the farm. In the background is the plight of the Japanese farmer who, on the average, owns less than three acres of farmland.

芥 川 龍 之 介

Born in Tokyo on 1 March 1892, Akuta-gawa distinguished himself early as an extraordinarily brilliant student. He majored in English at Tokyo University and translated works of such writers as Anatole France and W.B. Yeats, but he was also widely read in the Japanese classics. While he was still an under-graduate he wrote the short stories 'Rashōmon' and 'The Nose,' the latter of which brought him high critical ac-claim. After graduation he taught Eng-lish at Navy Engineering School near Tokyo for about two years. It was during this time that he began writing haiku in earnest, using the pseudonym Gaki. In 1919 he started working for the news-paper *Mainichi*; his assignments were to write short stories and essays. In 1921 he visited China for five months. From about that time his health began to deteriorate, and he suffered several nervous break-downs. Finally on 24 July 1927, when he was just thirty-five, he took an overdose of sleeping pills and died. Among his noted works are 'The Handkerchief' (1916), 'Hell Screen' (1918), 'Flatcar' (1922), and *Kappa* (1927), besides the two short stories mentioned above.

The day autumn began
I had a cavity in my tooth
filled with silver.

White chrysanthemums:
in the fragrance, too, there are
light and shade.

秋 立 つ 日 う ろ 歯 に 銀 を う づ め け り
Aki / tatsu / hi / uroba / ni / gin / o / uzume-keri
Autumn | starting | day | hollow-tooth | in | silver | (acc.) | fill-keri

---

白 菊 や 匂 に も あ る 影 日 な た
Shiragiku / ya / nioi / ni / mo / aru / kage / hinata
White-chrysanthemums | : | fragrance | in | also | there-are | shade | light

Wintry gusts:
on the sardine still lingers
the ocean's colour.

The butterfly's tongue
resembles a steel spring—
what a hot day!

木 が ら し や 目 刺 に の こ る 海 の い ろ
Kogarashi / ya / mezashi / ni / nokoru / umi-no / iro
Wintry-gusts | : | *sardine* | *on* | *remains* | *sea's* | *colour*

蝶 の 舌 ゼ ン マ イ に 似 る 暑 さ か な
Chō-no / shita / zenmai / ni / niru / atsusa / kana
Butterfly's | *tongue* | *spring* | *to* | *resembling* | *hotness* | kana

Green frog,
have you also had your body
freshly painted?

An ant lion's pit
is hidden underneath a peony
blossoming in red.

青蛙おのれもペンキ塗りたてか
Aogaeru / onore / mo / penki / nuritate / ka
Green-frog | you | also | paint | freshly-painted | ?

蟻地獄陰して牡丹花赤き
Arijigoku / kage / shite / botan / hana / akaki
Ant-lion's-pit | shade | making | peony | flower | red

Sick and feverish
in the gleam of cherry blossoms
I keep shivering.

The moon above the hill
is serene; under it the smell
of fallen leaves.

熱 を 病 ん で 桜 明 り に 震 へ ゐ る
Netsu / o / yande / sakura / akari / ni / furue / iru
Fever / (acc.) / afflicted-with / cherry-blossoms / light / in / shivering / am

山 の 月 冴 え て 落 葉 の 匂 か な
Yama-no / tsuki / saete / ochiba-no / nioi / kana
Mountain's / moon / being-clear / fallen-leaves' / smell / kana

The red lily's pistil
darkens as the hot spell
reaches its peak.

The wind of autumn:
a hair has begun to grow
on my mole.

赤 百 合 の 蕊 黒 む 暑 さ 極 り ぬ
Akayuri-no / shibe / kuromu / atsusa / kiwamarinu
Red-lily's | pistil | darkens | hotness | has-culminated

秋 風 や 黒 子 に 生 え し 毛 一 根
Akikaze / ya / hokuro / ni / haeshi / ke / ikkon
Autumn-wind | : | mole | on | has-grown | hair | one

---

*Wind through the pine trees:
in the moonlight someone
digs truffles.*

*To the sweltering sky
it rises and disappears:
dust from the winnowing.*

松 風 や 人 は 月 下 に 松 露 を 堀 る
Matsukaze / ya / hito / wa / gekka / ni / shōro / o / horu
Pine-wind | : | person | as-for | under-the-moon | in | truffle | (acc.) | digs

炎 天 に 上 り て 消 え る 箕 の 埃
Enten / ni / noborite / kieru / mi-no / hokori
Flaming-sky | to | rising | vanishes | winnow's | dust

Slime on the stones—
gloomily through the water
the rays of the sun.

Branches of a tree
touching the tiles of the roof—
how hot it is!

石 の 垢 も の の う き 水 の 日 ざ し か な
Ishi-no / aka / monouki / mizu-no / hizashi / kana
Stones' / slime / melancholy / water's / sunlight / kana

木 の 枝 の 瓦 に さ は る 暑 さ か な
Ki-no / eda-no / kawara / ni / sawaru / atsusa / kana
Tree's / branches' / tiles / on / touch / hotness / kana

Unable to stand
with the stillness, it falls —
summer camellia.

Early autumn —
as I grab a grasshopper,
how soft it feels!

静 か さ に 堪 え ず 散 り け り 夏 椿
Shizukasa / ni / taezu / chiri-keri / natsu-tsubaki
Stillness | with | not-bearing | falls-keri *| summer-camellia*

初 秋 の 蝗 つ か め ば 柔 か き
Hatsuaki-no / inago / tsukameba / yawarakaki
Early-autumn's | grasshopper | when-grab | soft
AUTHOR'S HEADNOTE   *'Try to understand the thoughts of a haiku poet wearing a dark suit and a gray soft hat.'* A
thin man, Akutagawa is probably comparing himself to a grasshopper here.

The wind of autumn:
only the carapace remains
of a crab on the tray.

Even the rabbit
droops one of her ears—
midsummer heat!

秋 風 や 甲 羅 を あ ま す 膳 の 蟹
Akikaze / ya / kōra / o / amasu / zen-no / kani
Autumn-wind | : | carapace | (acc.) | leaves | tray's | crab

兎 も 片 耳 垂 る る 大 暑 か な
Usagi / mo / kata-mimi / taruru / taisho / kana
Rabbit | even | one-ear | droops | great-heat | kana

Under the bright sky
a hairy caterpillar crawls
on the pine tree's branch.

My runny nose:
everywhere, except on that spot,
evening dusk falls.

うららかに毛虫わたるや松の枝
Uraraka-ni / kemushi / wataru / ya / matsu-no / eda
Brightly | hairy-caterpillar | passes | : | pine's | branch

水洟や鼻の先だけ暮れ残る
Mizubana / ya / hana-no / saki / dake / kure-nokoru
Snivel | : | nose's | tip | only | remains-undarkened
Entitled 'Deriding Myself.' The night before his suicide Akutagawa handed this poem to his aunt, asking her to give it to his family doctor (who was an amateur haiku poet) the following morning.

飯 田 蛇 笏

Dakotsu was born on 26 April 1885, in a village near Mt Fuji, where his father was one of the largest landowners in the district. He went to Tokyo as a youngster and studied English literature at Waseda University. He wrote short stories and western-style poems in his college days. In 1909 he gave up school, sold all his books, and returned to his native village. In that peaceful environment he devoted his time to the writing of haiku. He soon became the editor of a local haiku magazine, *Isinglass,* and elevated it to one of the finest publications of its kind. With no need to work for his livelihood, he often travelled; he visited China and Korea in 1940. His wanderings resulted in poems, essays, and travel sketches. The years from 1941 to 1946 marked a dark period in his personal life, as he lost both his parents and three sons in succession. His creative activities, however, continued as vigorously as ever. He published nine books of haiku, including *Collection of Poems at a Mountain Hut* (1932), *Collection of Mountain Echoes* (1940), *Spring Orchids* (1947), and *Snowy Valleys* (1951). As these titles show, many of his poems reflect his reclusive life in his mountain village. He died on 3 October 1962.

White chrysanthemums—
how cold the dewdrops are
on my garden shears!

Before my eyes
a hollyhock; on it a snake.
I wake from a nap.

白 菊 の し づ く つ め た し 花 鋏
Shiragiku-no / shizuku / tsumetashi / hana-basami
White-chrysanthemums' | drops | are-cold | garden-shears

眼 近 く の 葵 に 蛇 や 昼 寝 覚
Majikaku-no / aoi / ni / hebi / ya / hirune-zame
Eye-proximity's | hollyhock | on | snake | : | waking-from-nap

---

How white the peonies
as I stop sermonizing
and free my eyes!

To the Sea of Death
it plunged with a splash—
a tiger moth.

牡丹しろし人倫を説く眼はなてば
Botan / shiroshi / jinrin / o / toku / me / hanateba
Peonies | are-white | ethics | (acc.) | preaching | eyes | when-release

---

幽冥へおつるおとあり灯取虫
Yūmei / e / otsuru / oto / ari / hitorimushi
Nether-world | to | falling | sound | there-is | tiger-moth
Yūmei, *the Land of the Dead, here refers to a light trap, a shallow oil-filled pan with a burning wick in its centre.*
Attracted by the light, moths come and fall into the pan.

Sick unto death,
how lovely her fingernails
on the wooden brazier!

For the hydrangea
August mountains are never
sufficiently high.

死 病 え て 爪 う つ く し き 火 桶 か な
Shibyō / ete / tsume / utsukushiki / hioke / kana
Mortal-illness / getting / fingernails / beautiful / wooden-brazier / kana

紫 陽 花 に 八 月 の 山 た か か ら ず
Ajisai / ni / hachigatsu-no / yama / takakarazu
Hydrangea / for / August's / mountains / are-not-high

In the setting sun
cocks are engaged in a duel:
touch-me-nots in bloom.

My soul moves along
quietly among the flowers—
a chrysanthemum exhibit.

落日に蹴合へる鶏や鳳仙花
Rakujitsu / ni / keaeru / tori / ya / hōsenka
Setting-sun | in | kicking-one-another | cocks | : | touch-me-nots

たましひのしづかにうつる菊見かな
Tamashii-no / shizuka-ni / utsuru / kikumi / kana
Soul's | quietly | moves | chrysanthemum-viewing | kana

A mosquito's whine:
in the depth of night I peer
into a hanging mirror.

As the moon has sunk
they fly round the Big Dipper—
the plovers.

蚊 の 声 や 夜 深 く の ぞ く 掛 け 鏡
Ka-no / koe / ya / yo / fukaku / nozoku / kakekagami
Mosquito's | voice | : | night | deep | peer | hanging-mirror

月 入 れ ば 北 斗 を め ぐ る 千 鳥 か な
Tsuki / ireba / hokuto / o / meguru / chidori / kana
Moon | as-set | Big-Dipper | (acc.) | go-round | plovers | kana

Out for a swim:
the water that drowns people
smells fragrant to me.

In the extreme cold
not a particle of dust
on the towering rock.

游 泳 や お ぼ る る 水 の か ん ば し き
Yūei / ya / oboruru / mizu-no / kanbashiki
Swimming | : | drowning | water's | fragrant

極 寒 の ち り も と ど め ず 厳 ぶ す ま
Gokkan-no / chiri / mo / todomezu / iwa-busuma
Extreme-cold's | dust | even | not-retaining | rock-screen

The eyes of a horse
that lost the race—how intently
they stare at men.

Snow-covered mountains—
crawling about for a long while,
echoes and re-echoes.

負馬の眼のまじまじと人を視る
Make-uma-no / me-no / maji-maji / to / hito / o / miru
Defeated-horse's / eyes' / stare-stare / thus / people / (acc.) / look-at

雪山をはひまはりゐるこだまかな
Setsuzan / o / hai-mawari / iru / kodama / kana
Snow-mountains / (acc.) / crawling-about / are / echoes / kana

In winter, a toad.
I set it free in the river —
it begins to swim!

                                        High noon in summer:
                                        Death, with half-closed eyes,
                                        observes a man.

冬 の 蟇 川 に は な て ば お よ ぎ け り
Fuyu-no / hiki / kawa / ni / hanateba / oyogi-keri
Winter's / *toad* / *river* / *in* / *when-release* / *swims*-keri

夏 真 昼 死 は 半 眼 に 人 を み る
Natsu / mahiru / shi / wa / hangan / ni / hito / o / miru
Summer / *high-noon* / *death* / *as-for* / *half-eye* / *with* / *man* / *(acc.)* / *looks-at*

No creature is there—
and yet, deep in the thawing stream,
I have seen a stir.

                                        His life has ended—
                                        the medicine's smell coldly
                                        leaves the body.

な に も ゐ ぬ 雪 水 ふ か く う ご き け り
Nani-mo / inu / yuki-mizu / fukaku / ugoki-keri
Anything | there-is-not | snow-water | deeply | moves-keri

い の ち つ き て 薬 香 さ む く は な れ け り
Inochi / tsukite / yakukō / samuku / hanare-keri
Life | ending | medicine-smell | coldly | parts-keri
Written on the death of the author's father in 1943.

In my forefathers' land
darkness rests in calm
this New Year's Eve.

The perfectly still
earth, with eyes almost closed,
enters on winter.

父 祖 の 地 に 闇 の し づ ま る 大 晦 日
Fuso-no / chi / ni / yami-no / shizumaru / ōmisoka
Forefathers' | land | in | darkness's | quieting-down | year's-last-day

---

凪 ぎ わ た る 地 は う す 眼 し て 冬 に 入 る
Nagi-wataru / chi / wa / usume / shite / fuyu / ni / iru
Calm-all-over| earth | as-for | thin-eyes | making | winter | on | enters

---

尾 崎 放 哉

Hōsai was born on 20 January 1885 in Tottori and received his early education there. In 1902 he went to Tokyo and entered the First National High School, where he met Ogiwara Seisensui and began writing haiku. At Tokyo University he majored in law, but he was more interested in philosophy, literature, and religion. He often visited a Zen temple in Kamakura. In 1911 he started working for a Tokyo-based insurance firm, and shortly afterwards he married a young woman from his home town. With a degree from Tokyo University he was one of the elite employees of the company, but apparently his work suffered as a result of his habitual drinking. He left the company in 1922 and tried to re-start his professional life at a new insurance firm in Korea the following year.

His attempt was short-lived, however, and, as he wandered in frustration through northern China, he became ill and had to return to Japan. That winter he decided to change the course of his life completely. He gave up all his belongings, persuaded his wife to leave him, and entered monastic life in Kyoto. Overanxious to attain his spiritual aim, he restlessly moved from one monastery to another, earning a minimum livelihood by doing chores at each place. Finally he settled down in a humble hut on a small island in the Seto Inland Sea, but soon afterwards he contracted tuberculosis, from which he never recovered. He died on 7 April 1926, just before his only collection of haiku was published.

At a crematorium
I look high up
towards the chimney's
immensity.

Into the evening sun
with all my strength
I chase a horse.

焼 き 場 の 煙 突 の 大 い さ を あ ふ ぐ
Yakiba-no / entotsu-no / ōisa / o / augu
Crematorium's | chimney's | largeness | (acc.) | look-up

夕 日 の 中 へ 力 い つ ぱ い 馬 を 追 い か け る
Yūhi / no-naka-e / chikara-ippai / uma / o / oikakeru
Evening-sun | into | with-full-strength | horse | (acc.) | chase

---

A pomegranate
has opened its mouth—
an idiotic
love affair.

Throughout the day
I did not speak a word:
the shadow of a butterfly
falls.

柘 榴 が 口 あ け た た は け た 恋 だ
Zakuro / ga / kuchi / aketa / tawaketa / koi / da
Pomegranate | (nomin.) | mouth | has-opened | idiotic | love | is

一 日 物 云 は ず 蝶 の 影 さ す
Ichi-nichi / mono / iwazu / chō-no / kage / sasu
All-day | thing | not-speak | butterfly's | shadow | falls

In the darkness of a well
I recognize my face.

Trying to cast away
a slanderous heart
I shell the beans.

井 戸 の 暗 さ に わ が 顔 を 見 出 す
Ido-no / kurasa / ni / waga / kao / o / miidasu
Well's | darkness | in | my | face | (acc.) | find

人 を そ し る 心 を す て 豆 の 皮 む く
Hito / o / soshiru / kokoro / o / sute / mame-no / kawa / muku
Person | (acc.) | slandering | heart | (acc.) | discarding | beans' | shells | remove

The crow
without saying a word
flew away.

Late at night
a sliding door
in the distance
is closed.

烏 が だ ま つ て と ん で 行 つ た
Karasu / ga / damatte / tonde / itta
Crow / (nomin.) / silently / flying / has-gone

夜 中 の 襖 遠 く し め ら れ た る
Yonaka-no / fusuma / tōku / shimeraretaru
Midnight's / sliding-door / far-away / has-been-closed

The sky above a mountain graveyard
in the evening sun
slants towards the ocean.

From a lonely body
fingernails begin to grow.

山 の 夕 陽 の 墓 地 の 空 海 へ か た ぶ く
Yama-no / yūhi-no / bochi-no / sora / umi / e / katabuku
Mountain's | evening-sun's | graveyard's | sky | sea | to | slants

---

淋 し い か ら だ か ら 爪 が の び 出 す
Sabishii / karada / kara / tsume / ga / nobi-dasu
Lonely | body | from | fingernails | (nomin.) | begin-to-grow

---

In the hollow mind
a pair of eyes
opens.

Spring is here—
so says a spacious
newspaper ad.

うつろの心に眼が二つあいてゐる
Utsurono / kokoro / ni / me / ga / futatsu / aite-iru
Hollow | heart | in | eyes | (nomin.) | two | are-open

春が来たと大きな新聞広告
Haru / ga / kita / to / ōkina / shinbun-kōkoku
Spring | (nomin.) | has-come | thus | large | newspaper-advertisement

---

The festival:
a baby
is asleep.

Splendid breasts—
there is a mosquito.

お 祭 り 赤 ん 坊 寝 て ゐ る
Omatsuri / akanbō / nete-iru
Festival / baby / is-sleeping

す ば ら し い 乳 房 だ 蚊 が 居 る
Subarashii / chibusa / da / ka / ga / iru
Splendid / breasts / are / mosquito / (nomin.) / there-is

Moonlit night:
a reed
is broken.

An ailing person
watches
a flower
being cut.

月 夜 の 葦 が 折 れ と る
Tsukiyo-no / ashi / ga / ore-toru
Moonlight-night's | reed | (nomin.) | is-broken

切 ら れ る 花 を 病 人 見 て ゐ る
Kirareru / hana / o / byōnin / mite-iru
Being-cut | flower | (acc.) | sick-person | is-watching

As I wash the sole of my foot
it becomes white.

With the flow of the stream
I walk
and pause.

足 の う ら 洗 へ ば 白 く な る
Ashi-no / ura / araeba / shiroku / naru
Foot's | backside | when-wash | white | becomes

流 れ に 沿 う て 歩 い て と ま る
Nagare / ni / sōte / aruite / tomaru
Flow | with | along | walking | stop

---

*The footsteps of a sparrow
walking on the tatami floor
sound familiar.*

                                        *To the back of a tombstone
                                        I go round.*

畳 を 歩 く 雀 の 足 音 を 知 つ て 居 る
Tatami / o / aruku / suzume-no / ashioto / o / shitte-iru
Tatami (straw) mat | (acc.) | treading | sparrow's | foot-sound | (acc.) | know

---

墓 の う ら に 廻 る
Haka-no / ura / ni / mawaru
Tombstone's | backside | to | go-round

日 野 草 城

Born in Tokyo on 18 July 1901, Sōjō spent most of his boyhood in Korea, as his father worked there. In 1918 he entered a junior college in Kyoto and soon became the colourful leader of the student haiku club. He then proceeded to Kyoto University, where he studied law. Upon graduation in 1924 he joined a large insurance company in Osaka. His position in the company rose with the years, until he reached the coveted post of Kobe branch manager in 1945. His literary activities, however, gradually abated as Japan's wartime policy put more and more strictures on writers and poets. In 1945 he lost most of his belongings in an air raid. The following year he took to bed with pneumonia, pleurisy, and waxy disease of the lungs. His illness worsened steadily in the difficult years that followed the war. His right lung virtually stopped functioning, and then his right eye went blind. After years of bedridden life at his home near Osaka, he died on 29 January 1956. He had written eight volumes of haiku.

Spring evening's lamplight:
a woman; she does not have
an Adam's apple.

Seeds of some sort—
grasping them, I feel the jostle
of lives against my palm.

春 の 灯 や 女 は 持 た ぬ の ど ぼ と け
Haru-no / hi / ya / onna / wa / motanu / nodobotoke
Spring's | lamp | : | woman | as-for | has-not | Adam's-apple

---

物 種 を 握 れ ば 生 命 ひ し め け る
Mono-dane / o / nigireba / inochi / hishimekeru
Some-seeds | (acc.) | when-grasp | life | jostling

Early spring dawn:
nobody else would know of
this rain on the trees.

Wintry gusts:
abortion-herb is boiling
and yet ... and yet ...

春暁や人こそ知らね木々の雨
Shungyō / ya / hito / koso / shirane / kigi-no / ame
Spring-dawn | : | people | (emph.) | not-know | trees' | rain

---

凩や堕胎草煮は煮たれども
Kogarashi / ya / oroshi-gusa / ni / wa / ni-tare / domo
Wintry-gusts | : | abortion-herb | boiling | as-for | has-boiled | yet

---

The morning cold:
smelling of tooth powder,
my wife's mouth.

My pondering
turns into the moonlight,
filling the sky.

朝 寒 や 歯 磨 匂 ふ 妻 の 口
Asa-samu / ya / hamigaki / niou / tsuma-no / kuchi
Morning-cold | : | tooth-powder | smelling | wife's | mouth

わ が 思 ひ 月 か げ と な り 空 に 満 つ
Waga / omoi / tsukikage / to / nari / sora / ni / mitsu
My | musing | moonlight | to | turning | sky | in | is-filled

---

The grebe
when it becomes lonely
dives into the water.

I close my eyes
and bask in the warmth of love
that is long past.

かいつぶりさびしくなればくぐりけり
Kaitsuburi / sabishiku / nareba / kuguri-keri
Dabchick | lonely | when-becomes | dives-keri

眼をとぢてむかしの恋にあたたまる
Me / o / tojite / mukashi-no / koi / ni / atatamaru
Eyes | (acc.) | closing | long-past's | love | in | get-warm

At a flash of lightning
they blinked their eyes—
the leafless trees.

She sulks,
says nothing, and becomes
a white rose.

いなづまにまばたきしたる枯木達
Inazuma / ni / mabataki / shi-taru / kareki-tachi
Lightning | at | blink | have-made | bare-trees

ひと拗ねてものいはず白き薔薇となる
Hito / sunete / mono / iwazu / shiroki / bara / to / naru
Person | sulking | thing | not-say | white | rose | to | turns

---

The fever is gone.
In the immeasurable void,
yellow weariness.

The morning-glory:
like fulfilled desire
it withers away.

熱 退 き ぬ 空 漠 と し て 黄 の 疲 弊
Netsu / hikinu / kūbaku / to / shite / ki-no / tsukare
Fever | has-ebbed | vast-void | thus | making | yellow's | weariness

朝 顔 や お も ひ を 遂 げ し ご と し ぼ む
Asagao / ya / omoi / o / togeshi / goto / shibomu
Morning-glory | : | desire | (acc.) | has-attained | like | withers

Moon sixteen nights old:
my urine glass glitters
at the veranda's edge.

A night watchman
strikes his clappers—at the sound
cracks run up the moonlight.

十六夜や溲瓶かがやく縁の端
Izayoi / ya / shubin / kagayaku / en-no / hashi
Sixteenth-night-moon | : | urine-glass | shines | veranda's | edge

---

夜番析を打つ月光にひび走る
Yoban / ki / o / utsu / gekkō / ni / hibi / hashiru
Night-watchman | clappers | (acc.) | strikes | moonlight | in | crack | runs
Ki, *in this particular case, is a pair of small wooden blocks which a night watchman claps together to attract attention.*

My wife holds
a thistle—I feel its prickles
in my hand.

Dark summer night—
sick and feverish, I
emit a gleam.

妻 が 持 つ 薊 の 棘 を 手 に 感 ず
Tsuma / ga / motsu / azami-no / toge / o / te / ni / kanzu
Wife | (nomin.) | holds | thistle's | prickles | (acc.) | hand | in | feel

夏 の 闇 高 熱 の わ れ 発 光 す
Natsu / no / yami / kōnetsu-no / ware / hakkō-su
Summer's | darkness | high-fever's | I | emit-light

The weeds
are now beginning to wither,
and in peace, too.

The autumn road
enters the shade—and emerges
into the sunshine.

荒 草 の 今 は 枯 れ つ つ 安 ら か に
Arakusa-no / ima / wa / kare-tsutsu / yasuraka / ni
Weeds' / now / as-for / withering / peace / in

秋 の 道 日 か げ に 入 り て 日 に 出 で て
Aki-no / michi / hikage / ni / irite / hi / ni / idete
Autumn's / road / shade / into / entering / sun / into / going-out

Its sight has been lost
and yet, for that eye also
I polish the eyeglass.

It's the lilac's scent—
so I notice, and wake
from my noonday nap.

見えぬ眼の方の眼鏡の玉も拭く
Mienu / me-no / hō-no / megane-no / tama / mo / fuku
Sightless / eye's / side's / eyeglasses' / glass / also / wipe

リラの香と気づきて昼寝さめにけり
Rira-no / ka / to / kizukite / hirune / same-ni-keri
Lilac's / scent / thus / noticing / noonday-nap / have-waked-keri

水 原 秋桜子

Shūōshi was born in Tokyo on 9 October 1892. His father was a physician and operated a clinic. The eldest son, Shūōshi was to take over his father's work, so he studied medicine at Tokyo University. He specialized first in serology, and then in obstetrics and gynaecology, receiving an MD degree in 1926. In 1928 he became a professor at Showa Medical College in Tokyo, and later in the same year he began practising medicine at his father's clinic. In 1932 he was appointed medical advisor for the Ministry of the Imperial Household. He had begun writing poetry as an undergraduate student. He first wrote tanka, but soon turned to haiku.

His first volume of haiku, *Katsushika*, was published in 1930. The following year he disassociated himself from the *Cuckoo* poets and became the leader of a new haiku group which published the magazine *Staggerbush*. An energetic man, he has written nearly twenty volumes of haiku in the years since, including *Verdure* (1933), *Autumn Garden* (1935), *Old Mirror* (1942), *Frosty Grove* (1950), *Loneliness on a Journey* (1961), and *Martyrdom* (1969). After his retirement from medical practice in 1952 he travelled a great deal, often visiting old Buddhist temples that had had a special attraction for him ever since his student days. He lives in Tokyo.

How the mulberry leaves
shine, as I trudge along the way
towards my parents' home!

                                    Everywhere in sight
                                    reed tassels waver, as
                                    night begins to fall.

桑 の 葉 の 照 る に 堪 へ ゆ く 帰 省 か な
Kuwa-no / ha-no / teru / ni / tae / yuku / kisei / kana
Mulberry's | leaves' | shine | with | bearing | go | return-to-native-place | kana
The word kisei is often associated with a college student returning to his parents' home in the country on a vacation. Mulberry leaves, a familiar sight in the Japanese countryside, are large and deep green; they grow vigorously in the summer sun.

見 る か ぎ り 蘆 花 ゆ ら ぎ ゐ て 暮 る る か な
Miru / kagiri / roka / yuragi-ite / kururu / kana
See | as-far-as | reed-flowers | wavering | darkness | kana

As I look upward
mountain azaleas burn
above the lava.

I close the gate
and sit alone with the stones
this beautiful night.

見 あ ぐ る や 山 躑 躅 燃 ゆ 熔 岩 の 上
Mi-aguru / ya / yama-tsutsuji / moyu / raba-no / ue
Look-up | : | mountain-azaleas | burn | lava's | top

門 と ぢ て 良 夜 の 石 と 我 は 居 り
Mon / tojite / ryōya-no / ishi / to / ware / wa / ori
Gate | closing | beautiful-night's | stones | with | I | as-for | am

*A winter chrysanthemum
wears nothing—except its own
beams of light.*

*The distant past
recedes still farther, under
the radiant sun.*

冬菊のまとふはおのがひかりのみ
Fuyugiku-no / matou / wa / ono-ga / hikari / nomi
Winter-chrysanthemum's / wear / as-for / self's / light / only

遠き世は麗ら日の下になほ遠き
Tōki / yo / wa / urarabi-no / shita / ni / nao / tōki
Distant / age / as-for / bright-sun's / underneath / in / still / distant

---

Bush clover, a wind.
Something makes me hurry, and I
wonder what it is.

I wake from a dream
and am startled by the darkness:
evening in autumn.

萩 の 風 何 か 急 か る る 何 な ら む
Hagi-no / kaze / nani-ka / sekaruru / nani / naramu
Bush-clover's / wind / something / hurry / what / could-be

夢 さ め て お ど ろ く 闇 や 秋 の 暮
Yume / samete / odoroku / yami / ya / aki-no / kure
Dream / waking / startle / darkness / : / autumn's / evening

Where angels' images
have crumbled, early summer
butterflies swarm.

                              The gigantic dog
                              rises to receive a guest
                              in the darkness of May.

天 使 像 く だ け て 初 夏 の 蝶 群 れ を り
Tenshi-zō / kudakete / shoka-no / chō / mure-ori
Angel-images / crumbling / early-summer's / butterflies / swarming

---

巨 き 犬 立 ち 迎 え た る 五 月 闇
Ōki / inu / tachi / mukae-taru / satsuki-yami
Gigantic / dog / rising / has-received / May-darkness

Blown in the wind,
it is whiter than the waves—
lotus in autumn.

The disused canal—
what causes the waves to rise
in the snow?

吹 か れ て は 波 よ り し ろ し 秋 の 蓮
Fukarete / wa / nami / yori / shiroshi / aki-no / hasu
Being-blown / as-for / waves / more-than / is-white / autumn's / lotus

癈 運 河 何 に 波 立 つ 雪 の 中
Haiunga / nani / ni / nami / tatsu / yuki-no / naka
Disused-canal / what / at / waves / rise / snow's / inside

*Beyond a garden
of sunflowers, the mast of a boat
is yellow too.*

*Mountain moths do not
hover about a lamp; they
hover about the moon.*

向 日 葵 の 前 の 船 檣 も 黄 な り け り
Himawari-no / mae-no / masuto / mo / ki / nari-keri
Sunfllowers' | front's | mast | also | yellow | is-keri

山 の 蛾 は ラ ン プ に 舞 は ず 月 に 舞 ふ
Yama-no / ga / wa / ranpu / ni / mawazu / tsuki / ni / mau
Mountain's | moths | as-for | lamp | at | not-hovering | moon | at | hover

The morning clouds
make me sad, and I don't know why—
a crepe myrtle.

In the temple shrine
a peony blooms, or so
it seems, and I pray.

朝雲の故なくかなし百日紅
Asagumo-no / yue / naku / kanashi / sarusuberi
Morning-clouds' | reason | non-existent | am-sad | crepe-myrtle

廚子の中に芍薬咲くと見て拝む
Zushi-no / naka / ni / shakuyaku / saku / to / mite / ogamu
Temple-shrine's | inside | in | peony | blooms | thus | seeing | pray

As it grows cloudy
Buddhas turn their faces downwards—
tree frogs start to croak.

At midnight I wake
and hear the wind soliciting
an avalanche.

曇り来て諸仏面伏す雨蛙
Kumori-kite / shobutsu / omo / fusu / amagaeru
Becoming-cloudy | Buddhas | faces | droop | rain-frogs

夜半さめて雪崖をさそふ風聞けり
Yowa / samete / nadare / o / sasou / kaze / kikeri
Midnight | waking | avalanche | (acc.) | soliciting | wind | have-heard

A dead vine, swimming
in the river pool, tries
to reach the other shore.

Is this the smell
of rice plants? As I wonder,
the darkness rustles.

枯 蔓 の 泳 ぎ て 渕 を 越 え む と す
Karezuru-no / oyogite / fuchi / o / koemu / to / su
Dead-vine's | swimming | river-pool | (acc.) | will-cross | thus | attempts

稲 の 香 と お も ふ や 闇 の そ よ ぎ を り
Ine-no / ka / to / omou / ya / yami-no / soyogi-ori
Rice-plants' | smell | thus | think | that-instant | darkness's | rustling

山 口 誓 子

Seishi was born on 3 November 1901 in Kyoto, where his father was an electrical engineer. Seishi, however, spent much of his boyhood with his grandfather who headed a newspaper press in Sakhalin. After graduating from a junior college in Kyoto he entered Tokyo University to study law. In 1926 he received a Bachelor of Law degree and immediately began working for a large commercial firm in Osaka. He was, however, of a delicate constitution and had to take sick leave frequently, sometimes for extended periods. From 1941 on he lived a quiet life in rural towns on the Pacific coast in central Honshu, nursing his health. Haiku, which he had begun writing as a young student, provided a diversion for him throughout these years. He has published more than a dozen volumes of haiku: *Frozen Harbour* (1932), *Yellow Flag* (1935), *Turbulent Waves* (1946), *Evening Hours* (1947), *Japanese Clothes* (1955), *Direction* (1967), and others; he has written many books of essays as well. Today he lives in Nishinomiya, a residential city near Osaka, on the coast of the Seto Inland Sea.

On a July day
near the green mountains,
a smelting furnace.

With a crunching sound
the praying mantis devours
the face of a bee.

七月の青嶺まぢかく熔鉱炉
Shichigatsu-no / aone / majikaku / yōkōro
July's | green-mountains | close-by | smelting-furnace

かりかりと蟷螂蜂の貌を食む
Karikari / to / tōrō / hachi-no / kao / o / hamu
Karikari *(onomat.) | thus | praying-mantis | bee's | face | (acc.) | devours*

Amid the summer grass
the wheels of a steam engine
come to a standstill.

The spring tide:
piercing my entire body,
the whistle from a boat.

夏 草 に 汽 罐 車 の 車 輪 来 て 止 る
Natsukusa / ni / kikansha-no / sharin / kite / tomaru
Summer-grass | in | steam-engine's | wheels | coming | stop

春 潮 や わ が 総 身 に 船 の 汽 笛
Shunchō / ya / waga / sōshin / ni / fune-no / fue
Spring-tide | : | my | whole-body | in | boat's | whistle

River in summer—
a red iron chain, its end
soaking in the water.

An autumnal wind
passes by, and a little baby
opens an eye.

夏 の 河 赤 き 鉄 鎖 の は し 浸 る
Natsu-no / kawa / akaki / tessa-no / hashi / hitaru
Summer's | river | red | iron-chain's | end | soaks

秋 風 が 通 る に 嬰 児 片 眼 を あ き
Akikaze / ga / tōru / ni / eiji / katame / o / aki
Autumn-wind | (nomin.) | passes | on | infant | one-eye | (acc.) | opening

All alone, I hug
my knees ... an autumnal wind,
again, autumnal wind.

In the water jar
floats an ant, and its shadow
is not.

ひ と り 膝 を 抱 け ば 秋 風 ま た 秋 風
Hitori / hiza / o / dakeba / akikaze / mata / akikaze
Alone | knees | (acc.) | when-hug | autumn-wind | again | autumn-wind

水 甕 に 浮 べ る 蟻 の 影 は な く
Mizugame / ni / ukaberu / ari-no / kage / wa / naku
Water-jar | in | floating | ant's | shadow | as-for | non-existent

Was that a voice?
Back toward the sweltering sky
I turn my face.

                         Under the flaming sky,
                         a distant sail: in my
                         heart, a sail.

声 な り し や と 炎 天 を 顧 み る
Koe / narishi / ya / to / enten / o / kaerimiru
Voice / was / ? / thus / flaming-sky / (acc.) / look-back

炎 天 の 遠 き 帆 や わ が こ こ ろ の 帆
Enten-no / tōki / ho / ya / waga / kokoro-no / ho
Flaming-sky's / distant / sail / : / my / heart's / sail

The sunset glow:
changing my mind, I pick up
a seashell.

In the daytime I saw
an ant, and it haunts my mind
in this darkness of night.

夕焼や思ひかへして貝拾ふ
Yūyake / ya / omoi-kaeshite / kai / hirou
Evening-glow | : | changing-one's-mind | seashell | pick-up

昼見たる蟻を暗夜に思ひ出づ
Hiru / mi-taru / ari / o / anya / ni / omoiizu
Daytime | have-seen | ant | (acc.) | dark-night | in | recall

Delighted to be born
a girl, in the spring sun
she closes her eyes.

The gentleness
pervades its shell—
a snail.

少女たるよろこび春の日に瞑る
Shōjo / taru / yorokobi / haru-no / hi / ni / metsumuru
Girl | being | joy | spring's | sun | in | closes-eyes

やさしさは殻透くばかり蝸牛
Yasashisa / wa / kara / suku / bakari / katatsumuri
Gentleness | as-for | shell | pervades | so-much | snail

Passing in the sky
wild geese call; that instant,
a feel of the mid-air.

Into my midday nap,
again and again, someone
hammers a nail.

行 く 雁 の 啼 く と き 宙 の 感 ぜ ら れ
Yuku / kari-no / naku / toki / chū-no / kanzerare
Going | wild-geese's | call | when | mid-air's | is-felt

昼 寝 の 中 し ば し ば 釘 を 打 ち 込 ま る
Hirune-no / naka / shibashiba / kugi / o / uchikomaru
Midday-nap's | inside | frequently | nail | (acc.) | is-hammered-in

Evening in autumn—
under the water also
it becomes dark.

In the waves no trace
remains, though I have swum there
with a woman.

秋 の 暮 水 中 も ま た 暗 く な る
Aki-no / kure / suichū / mo-mata / kuraku / naru
Autumn's-evening | in-the-water | also | dark | becomes

浪 に あ と か た も な し 女 と 泳 ぎ し が
Nami / ni / atokata / mo / nashi / onna / to / oyogishi / ga
Waves | in | trace | even | is-non-existent | woman | with | have-swum | but

Since they died
darkness fills up the space
in the firefly cage.

In the winter river
a whole sheet of newspaper,
soaked through, floating.

死 に け れ ば 闇 た ち こ む る 螢 籠
Shini-kereba / yami / tachikomuru / hotaru-kago
As-die-keri / darkness / fills-up / firefly-cage

冬 河 に 新 聞 全 紙 浸 り 浮 く
Fuyu-kawa / ni / shinbun / zenshi / tsukari / uku
Winter-river / in / newspaper / whole-sheet / soaking / floats

---

富 安 風 生

Fūsei was born on 16 April 1885 in a village near Nagoya. His grandfather and an older brother were amateur haiku poets, so he was exposed to poetry from early in life. He studied law at Tokyo University, graduating in 1910. He then entered the civil service and worked in the Ministry of Communications. He held various high administrative posts there, eventually becoming the Deputy Minister of Communications in 1936. He started to write haiku seriously in about 1918, when he was stationed in Kyushu.

With some of his colleagues in government service he initiated a literary magazine called *Young Leaves* and in 1928 became the editor of its haiku pages. In 1937 he retired from the civil service and began to spend more time travelling and writing haiku, though at times he was called back by the government to serve on important national committees. He has published twelve volumes of haiku, among them *Flowers of Grass* (1933), *Wind through the Pine Trees* (1940), *Village Life* (1947), *Evening Cool* (1955), and *Since My Eightieth Birthday* (1968). He lives in Tokyo.

Under the sky,
brightened by a large fire,
a washing basin.

To the falling shreds
of blossoms a carp opens its mouth:
summer has come.

大 火 事 に 明 る き 空 や 手 水 鉢
Ōkaji / ni / akaruki / sora / ya / chōzubachi
Large-fire | with | bright | sky | : | washing-basin

花 屑 に 口 開 く 鯉 や 夏 め き て
Hana-kuzu / ni / kuchi / aku / koi / ya / natsu-mekite
Flower-rubbish | at | mouth | opens | carp | : | being-summerlike

The morning cold:
a steam engine passes
warmly before my face.

After deciding
which way to turn, a berry
begins to float down.

朝 寒 や 汽 鑵 車 ぬ く く 顔 を 過 ぐ
Asazamu / ya / kikansha / nukuku / kao / o / sugu
Morning-cold | : | steam-engine | warmly | face | (acc.) | passes

---

向 き 定 め て 流 れ そ め た る 木 の 実 か な
Muki / kimete / nagare / some-taru / ko-no-mi / kana
Direction | deciding | flowing | has-begun | berry | kana

Silver Pavilion—
in the paddy before its gate,
a scarecrow.

At a western-style house
Japanese dishes are served:
blossoms on a pine tree.

銀 閣 寺 門 前 の 田 の 案 山 子 か な
Ginkakuji / monzen-no / ta-no / kakashi / kana
Silver-Pavilion | gate-front's | paddy's | scarecrow | kana
Ginkakuji *is the famous Temple of the Silver Pavilion located in Kyoto. It was built in the fifteenth century.*

洋 館 の 日 本 料 理 や 松 の 花
Yōkan-no / Nihon-ryōri / ya / matsu-no / hana
Western-style-house's | Japanese-dishes | : | pine's | blossoms

---

Into the miniature
garden a sick leaf has fallen,
and how large it is!

                              Butterflies fly low
                              because the hollyhock
                              flowers are low.

箱 庭 に 病 葉 落 ち て 大 い な り
Hakoniwa / ni / byōyō / ochite / ōinari
Miniature-garden | into | sick-leaf | having-fallen | is-large

---

蝶 低 し 葵 の 花 の 低 け れ ば
Chō / hikushi / aoi-no / hana-no / hikukereba
Butterflies | are-low | hollyhocks' | flowers' | as-are-low

As I rejoice
they fall time and time again:
nuts from the tree.

Sweeping off the acorns
is all I need to do, when
cleaning the graves.

よろこべばしきりに落つる木の実かな
Yorokobeba / shikirini / otsuru / ko-no-mi / kana
When-rejoice / *frequently* / *fall* / *nuts* / *kana*

樫の実を掃くばかりなり墓掃除
Kashi-no / mi / o / haku / bakari / nari / haka-sōji
Oak's / *nuts* / *(acc.)* / *sweep* / *only* / *is* / *grave-cleaning*

Waving handkerchiefs,
they even enjoy a parting:
the young maidens.

The full moon, for
a moment, looked misshapen
and I wonder why.

ハンケチ振つて別れも愉し少女等は
Hankechi / futte / wakare / mo / tanoshi / otome-ra / wa
Handkerchiefs | waving | parting | even | is-enjoyable | maidens | as-for

望月のふと歪みしと見しはいかに
Mochizuki-no / futo / yugamishi / to / mishi / wa / ikani
Full-moon's | momentarily | has-become-wry | thus | have-seen | as-for | why

I read a book—
somewhere within the book
an insect chirps.

At the gas station
a bright red Pegasus—
spring rain.

本 読 め ば 本 の 中 よ り 虫 の 声
Hon / yomeba / hon-no / naka / yori / mushi-no / koe
Book / when-read / book's / inside / from / insect's / voice

ガ ソ リ ン の 真 赤 き 天 馬 春 の 雨
Gasorin-no / ma-akaki / tenba / haru-no / ame
Gasoline's / bright-red / Pegasus / spring's / rain

All over the water
fallen blossoms spread, and amongst them
a frog's eyes.

Before a great many
people's eyes a solitary
tinted leaf falls.

一めんの落花の水に蛙の眼
Ichimen-no / rakka-no / mizu / ni / kaeru-no / me
Whole-surface's / fallen-blossoms' / water / on / frog's / eyes

---

多勢の眼に一片の散紅葉
Ōzei-no / me / ni / hitohira-no / chiri-momiji
Large-crowd's / eyes / in / one / falling-coloured-leaf

It totters too —
a moth, under the stillness
of the grove.

A lily stalk
concentrating all its might
into one flower bud.

よろぼへる蛾も林中の閑かさに
Yoroboeru / ga / mo / rinchū-no / shizukasa / ni
Totters | moth | also | grove-interior's | stillness | at

一茎の百合の全力一蕾に
Ikkei-no / yuri-no / zenryoku / ichirai / ni
One-stalk's | lily's | all-strength | one-bud | into

Like a father
and also like a mother,
the huge summer tree.

After giving birth
to a full moon, lakeside mountains
breathe in and out.

父 の ご と ま た 母 の ご と 大 夏 木
Chichi / no-goto / mata / haha / no-goto / ō-natsuki
Father / like / also / mother / like / large-summer-tree

満 月 を 生 み し 湖 山 の 息 づ か ひ
Mangetsu / o / umishi / kozan-no / ikizukai
Full-moon / (acc.) / having-given-birth / lakeside-mountains' / breathing

川 端 茅 舎

Bōsha was born in Tokyo on 14 August 1900, according to the official family registry (although his half-brother believed his birthdate was 17 August 1897). His father was an amateur painter, calligrapher, and haiku poet; as a result Bōsha also developed artistic interests early in his boyhood. He first wanted to be a painter and became a disciple of a leading oil painter of the time, though he also liked to write haiku and had some of his works accepted by the *Cuckoo* when he was in his late teens. When his father began operating a geisha house, young Bōsha was repelled and longed for a hermit's life. He often visited Buddhist temples for meditation. When his family home was destroyed in the great earthquake of 1923, he parted with his parents to enter a Zen monastery in Kyoto, where he spent the next several years. However he had to give up his training both in Zen and in painting when his health deteriorated. A sickly person since his early twenties, he contracted caries of the spine in 1931 and was confined to bed for most of his life thereafter. Haiku became his sole preoccupation, and he kept writing to the very end of his life. He died on 17 July 1941. *The Haiku of Kawabata Bōsha, a Definitive Edition* was published in 1946.

From the monks' cells
a smell of cooking meat:
autumn leaves at nightfall.

Like a diamond
a drop of dew, all alone
on a stone.

院々の肉煮ゆる香や夕紅葉
In'in-no / niku / niyuru / ka / ya / yū / momiji
(Monks') cells' / meat / cooking / smell / : / evening / autumn-leaves

金剛の露ひとつぶや石の上
Kongō-no / tsuyu / hitotsubu / ya / ishi / no-ue
Diamond's / dew / one-drop / : / stone / on

A stem of knotweed
in his mouth, a young acolyte
sweeps the graveyard.

In the crystal beads
of my rosary young leaves
are mirrored.

虎 杖 を 啣 へ て 沙 弥 や 墓 掃 除
Itadori / o / kuwaete / shami / ya / haka-sōji
Giant-knotweed | (acc.) | holding-in-mouth | acolyte | : | graveyard-cleaning
The giant knotweed is edible. In spring children in rural Japan go knotweed hunting in the fields and hills.

水 晶 の 念 珠 に 映 る 若 葉 か な
Suishō-no / nenju / ni / utsuru / wakaba / kana
Crystal's | rosary | in | are-mirrored | young-leaves | kana

To the butterfly in the sky
all buildings on the temple ground
are upside down.

The horse loaded with turnips
has a Bodhisattva's face,
with tears in his eyes.

蝶 の 空 七 堂 伽 藍 さ か し ま に
Chō-no / sora / shichidō-garan / sakashima / ni
Butterfly's | sky | seven-temple-buildings | upside-down | in
Shichidō-garan *refers to the complex of buildings that constitutes a Buddhist cathedral. Normally there are seven principal buildings.*

大 根 馬 菩 薩 面 し て 眼 に な み だ
Daikon / uma / bosatsu-zura / shite / me / ni / namida
Turnips | horse | Bodhisattva-face | doing | eyes | in | tears

Nightfall on *a spring day:
in bed, I think longingly
of the gentle Bodhisattva.*

*The monk, a little
drunk, pats a friend on the head—
terrace in the moonlight.*

春 の 夜 や 寝 れ ば 恋 し き 観 世 音
Haru-no / yo / ya / nereba / koishiki / kanzeon
Spring's | night | : | when-go-to-bed | long-for | Kanzeon
Kanzeon *is Avalokitesvara, a female Bodhisattva embodying mercy. The spring night has romantic implications in the Japanese poetic tradition.*

僧 酔 う て 友 の 頭 撫 づ る 月 の 縁
Sō / yōte / tomo-no / zu / nazuru / tsuki-no / en
Monk | being-drunk | friend's | head | pats | moon's | terrace

---

Snow under the moon
is blue, dyeing with its blue
the darkness of night.

On a freezing night
to the Bodhisattva of Wisdom
I offer a candle.

月 の 雪 あ を あ を 闇 を 染 め に け り
Tsuki-no / yuki / ao-ao / yami / o / some-ni-keri
Moon's | snow | blue-blue | darkness | (acc.) | has-dyed-keri

---

氷 る 夜 の 文 珠 に 燭 を た て ま つ る
Kōru / yo-no / monju / ni / shoku / o / tatematsuru
Freezing | night's | Manjusri (Bodhisattva of Wisdom) | to | candle | (acc.) | offer

---

Now that the shower
has passed, the water spider
regains its halo.

The water spider
draws rings on the water, wherein
echoes a temple bell.

まひまひや雨後の円光とりもどし
Maimai / ya / ugo-no / enkō / torimodoshi
Water-spider / : / *after-rain* / *halo* / *regains*
The water spider circles round and round on the surface of the water. That circle is here likened to Buddha's halo.

まひまひの水輪に鐘の響かな
Maimai-no / minawa / ni / kane-no / hibiki / kana
Water-spider's / *water-rings* / *in* / *temple-bell's* / *echo* / *kana*

Carrying a halo
on its back, how impoverished
a mud snail!

Green onions flowering —
for a moment golden
Buddha was there.

光 輪 を 負 ひ て 貧 し き 田 螺 か な
Kōrin / o / oite / mazushiki / tanishi / kana
Light-ring | (acc.) | carrying-on-the-back | impoverished | mud-snail | kana

葱 の 花 ふ と 金 色 の 仏 か な
Negi-no / hana / futo / konjiki-no / hotoke / kana
Green-onions' | flowers | suddenly | gold-coloured | Buddha | kana
Green onions flower in late spring. The flower, white and ball-shaped, is called negibōzu *('onion monk') because the shape somewhat resembles a monk's shaven head.*

In the moonlight
how clearly the deep snow
shows its scars!

A spider web
hanging before my eyes, evening
mountains and rivers.

月 光 に 深 雪 の 創 の か く れ な し
Gekkō / ni / miyuki-no / kizu-no / kakure-nashi
Moonlight | in | deep-snow's | scars' | hide-not

眼 前 に 蜘 の 巣 か か り 夕 山 河
Ganzen-ni / kumo-no / su / kakari / yū / sanga
Before-one's-eyes | spider's | web | hanging | evening | mountains-rivers

In the shade of green
leaves the eyes of a black cat
glaring in gold.

Like a fireball, I
fall into a fit of coughing
in this hideout of mine.

緑 蔭 に 黒 猫 の 目 の か つ と 金
Ryokuin / ni / kuroneko-no / me-no / katto / kin
Green-shade | in | black-cat's | eyes' | fiercely | gold

火 の 玉 の 如 く に 咳 き て 隠 れ 栖 む
Hi-no / tama / no-gotoku-ni / sekite / kakure / sumu
Fire's | ball | like | coughing | hiding | live

As if it were my soul
a magnolia blooms out—
ailing, I feel better.

My head on a pillow
of stone, am I a cicada?
The weeping of rain...

我 が 魂 の ご と く 朴 咲 き 病 よ し
Waga / tama / no-gotoku / hō / saki / yamai / yoshi
My | soul | like | magnolia | blooming | illness | is-good

石 枕 し て わ れ 蟬 か 泣 き 時 雨
Ishi-makura / shite / ware / semi / ka / naki / shigure
Stone-pillow | doing | I | cicada | ? | weeping | winter-rain

Deathbed poem. Ishi makura may refer to a pillow made of porcelain (used for its cooling effect) or to an ordinary pillow which feels like stone to a dying man. The meaning of naki shigure is also ambiguous: it may be raining outside, or someone may be weeping at the bedside, or the dying poet may be imagining it all.

中 村 草 田 男

Kusatao was born in Amoy on 24 July 1901. His father was a career diplomat who lived overseas most of the time. Kusatao returned to Japan in 1904 and received elementary and secondary education in Matsuyama. In 1925 he went to Tokyo and majored in German literature at Tokyo University. As a student he was especially attracted to the works of Nietzsche, Hölderlin, Chekhov, Dostoevski, and Strindberg. Later he changed his major to Japanese literature and wrote his bachelor's thesis on Shiki. Completing his degree in 1933, he became a member of the teaching staff at the Seikei Gakuen schools in Tokyo. He taught there for the next thirty-four years, until he became professor emeritus in 1967. He began writing haiku in about 1928 and published his first volume of haiku, *The Eldest Son*, in 1936. He has since published six more collections, among them *Volcanic Island* (1939), *Past and Future* (1947), *Visit to My Mother's Native Place* (1956), and *Beautiful Farm* (1967). In 1946 he founded a haiku magazine called *Myriad Green Leaves* and has been its editor ever since. He has also written many essays and a few short stories which he called *märchen*. He lives in Tokyo.

Winter already—
too much like a signpost,
a gravestone.

An empty bottle
and an aged blind man
in the winter sunshine.

冬 す で に 路 標 に ま が ふ 墓 一 基
Fuyu / sudeni / rohyō / ni / magau / haka / ikki
Winter | already | signpost | for | is-taken | grave | one

空 瓶 と 老 い し 盲 の 冬 日 向
Akibin / to / oishi / mekura-no / fuyu / hinata
Empty-bottle | and | aged | blind-person's | winter | sunshine

---

Myriad green leaves—
in their midst my baby
begins to cut his teeth.

Ants in the nighttime:
the one that has lost its way
crawls in a circle.

万 緑 の 中 や 吾 子 の 歯 生 え 初 む る
Banryoku-no / naka / ya / ako-no / ha / hae / somuru
Ten-thousand-greens' | inside | : | my-child's | teeth | growing | begin

夜 の 蟻 迷 え る も の は 弧 を 描 く
Yoru-no / ari / mayoeru / mono / wa / ko / o / egaku
Night's | ants | lost | one | as-for | circle | (acc.) | draws

Things that do not possess
memories: freshly fallen snow
and a leaping squirrel.

When I plough
it moves; when I pause to rest
it is still—the earth.

記 憶 を 持 た ざ る も の 新 雪 と 跳 ぶ 栗 鼠 と
Kioku / o / motazaru / mono / shinsetsu / to / tobu / risu / to
Memories | (acc.) | not-have | things | new-snow | and | leaping | squirrel | and
AUTHOR'S NOTE *'My wife's father unexpectedly died at his temporary home in Shinano Province. At the news we*
rushed there at once.'

耕 せ ば う ご き 憩 え ば し づ か な 土
Tagayaseba / ugoki / ikoeba / shizukana / tsuchi
When-plough | moving | when-rest | still | earth

How I wish to live
forever! A woman's voice
and a cicada's cry.

In the sky there is
primeval blue, and from my wife
I receive an apple.

永 久 に 生 き た し 女 の 声 と 蟬 の 音 と
Towa / ni / ikitashi / onna-no / koe / to / semi-no / ne / to
Eternity | in | wish-to-live | woman's | voice | and | cicada's | sound | and

空 は 太 初 の 青 さ 妻 よ り 林 檎 う く
Sora / wa / taisho-no / aosa / tsuma / yori / ringo / uku
Sky | as-for | world's-beginning's | blue | wife | from | apple | receive
HEADNOTE *'Having lost my home, I live with my family at a room in the dormitory of the school I work for.'* Written
in 1946.

The metaphors are
gone, and so is my faith…
sun over a moor.

Scorching heat:
like a victory, the brightness
of the earth.

比 喩 も ろ と も 信 仰 消 え て 枯 野 の 日
Hiyu / morotomo / shinkō / kiete / kareno-no / hi
Metaphors / together-with / faith / vanishing / withered-moor's / sun

---

炎 熱 や 勝 利 の 如 き 地 の 明 る さ
Ennetsu / ya / shōri / no-gotoki / chi-no / akarusa
Scorching-heat / : / victory / like / earth's / brightness

Eating grapes—
like one word, another word,
and still another.

Appearing as if
nothing had happened, the brightness
of the midday sun.

葡 萄 食 ふ 一 語 一 語 の 如 く に て
Budō / kū / ichigo / ichigo / no-gotoku / nite
Grapes | eat | one-word | one-word | like | doing

何 事 も な か り し 如 き 日 盛 な り
Nanigoto / mo / nakarishi / gotoki / hizakari / nari
Anything | even | was-non-existent | like | high-noon | is

A water lily:
may something other than death
cleanse my body!

A plum blossom, trampled,
has become the insignia
of the earth.

睡 蓮 や 死 な ら ぬ も の 以 て 肉 浄 め よ
Suiren / ya / shi / naranu / mono / mote / niku / kiyome / yo
Water-lily | : | death | not-being | thing | with | flesh | cleanse | (imp.)

梅 一 輪 踏 ま れ て 大 地 の 紋 章 た り
Ume / ichirin / fumarete / daichi-no / monshō / tari
Plum-blossom | one | trampled | great-earth's | insignia | is

With a lizard
that droops its head, I listen
to the words of the sun.

Ten days after birth
the baby's life is reddish,
the wind is dazzling.

頭 を 伏 せ し 蜥 蜴 と 聴 け り 日 の 言 葉
Zu / o / fuseshi / tokage / to / kikeri / hi-ho / kotoba
Head | (acc.) | has-drooped | lizard | with | have-heard | sun's | words

生 れ て 十 日 生 命 が 赤 し 風 が ま ぶ し
Arate / tōka / inochi / ga / akashi / kaze / ga / mabushi
Being-born | ten-days | life | (nomin.) | is-red | wind | (nomin.) | is-dazzling

A cactus stood,
an evening crab scurried,
and I was born.

Each carrying a crescent
moon, water rings are anxious
to reach me!

覇 王 樹 立 ち 夕 蟹 走 り わ れ 生 れ し
Saboten / tachi / yūkani / hashiri / ware / areshi
Cactus | standing | evening-crab | running | I | was-born

三 日 月 の せ た 水 輪 こ ち ら へ 来 た が る よ
Mikazuki / noseta / mizuwa / kochira / e / kitagaru / yo
Crescent-moon | carrying | water-rings | this-way | to | wish-to-come | !

From inside a cabbage
the faint crow of a rooster—
vast and desolate.

The familiar scene
slowly strips off its darkness
as the New Year dawns.

玉 菜 の 芯 か ら 微 か な 鶏 鳴 広 漠 た り
Tamana-no / shin / kara / kasukana / keimei / kōbaku / tari
Cabbage's | core | from | faint | rooster's-crow | wide-desolate | is

旧 景 が 闇 を 脱 ぎ ゆ く 大 旦
Kyūkei / ga / yami / o / nugi-yuku / ō-ashita
Old-scene | (nomin.) | darkness | (acc.) | strips-off | New-Year's-dawn

石 田 波 郷

Born in Matsuyama on 18 March 1913, Hakyō attended the middle school where Shiki, Kyoshi, and Hekigodō had studied a generation earlier. Following in their footsteps, he began writing haiku while he was still young, and had them accepted by local newspapers for publication. In 1932 he went to Tokyo and joined Shūōshi's group, which was then preparing to publish the new haiku magazine *Staggerbush*. His first collection of haiku appeared in 1935, when he was only twenty-two. Two years later he started his own magazine called *Crane*.

His smooth progress to fame came to an abrupt halt in 1943, when he was drafted into the army and sent to northern China. After only a few months of army life he fell seriously ill with a lung ailment. He returned to Japan in 1945, but he never completely recovered from his illness. From 1948 to 1950 he was confined to bed at a hospital in Tokyo; he had a series of operations and more than one brush with death. Yet his desire to write poetry did not abate. In 1950 he published *Clinging to Life*, a collection of about five hundred haiku he had written during his illness. He died on 21 November 1969, after producing a total of seven volumes of haiku.

The caged eagle,
beginning to feel lonely,
flaps his wings.

Nightfall in autumn—
turning into flames of hellfire,
cornhusks burn.

檻 の 鷲 さ び し く な れ ば 羽 搏 つ か も
Ori-no | washi | sabishiku | nareba | ha | utsu | mako
Cage's | eagle | lonely | when-becomes | wings | beats | kamo

---

秋 の 暮 業 火 と な り て 秬 は 燃 ゆ
Aki-no | kure | gōka | to | narite | kibi | wa | moyu
Autumn's | evening | hellfire | to | turning | cornhusks | as-for | burn

In the cherry tree's buds
an intense force; looking upward
at them, I stagger.

Cicadas' morning—
all my loves and hatreds
have come back to me.

さくらの芽のはげしさ仰ぎ蹌めける
Sakura-no / me-no / hageshisa / aogi / yoromekeru
Cherry-tree's | buds' | intensity | looking-up | stagger

蟬の朝愛憎は悉く我に還る
Semi-no / asa / aizō / wa / kotogotoku / ware / ni / kaeru
Cicadas' | morning | love-hatred | as-for | all | me | to | return

On the frosty road
horse dung lies—I accept it,
and everything else.

In the morning cold
a streetcar begins to part
from soldiers and horses.

霜 の 道 馬 糞 そ の 他 を う べ な へ り
Shimo-no / michi / bafun / sono-ta / o / ubenaeri
Frost's / road / horse-dung / the-rest / (acc.) / accept

朝 寒 の 市 電 兵 馬 と 別 れ た り
Asa-samu-no / shiden / heiba / to / wakare-tari
Morning-cold's / streetcar / soldier-horse / with / has-parted
Written in 1940. Japan was at war, and one often saw an army troop marching along the city street, with a streetcar (loaded with civilians) following it slowly.

The morning-glory—
far beyond its dark blue,
months and days to come.

Freight trains, cold.
Hundreds and thousands of tombstones
trembling with them.

朝 顔 の 紺 の 彼 方 の 月 日 か な
Asagao-no / kon-no / kanata-no / tsukihi / kana
Morning-glory's / *dark-blue's* / *yonder* / *month-days* / kana

貨 車 寒 し 百 千 の 墓 う ち ふ る ひ
Kasha / samushi / hyaku / sen-no / haka / uchifurui
Freight-trains / *is-cold* / *hundreds* / *thousands'* / *tombs* / *trembling*

The butterfly, now dead,
floats across the flowing water
once again.

Amid the debris
perfectly transparent
midwinter water.

蝶 死 に て 流 る る 水 を 今 も 踰 ゆ
Chō / shinite / nagaruru / mizu / o / ima / mo / koyu
Butterfly / having-died / flowing / water / (acc.) / now / also / crosses

焼 跡 に 透 き と ほ り け り 寒 の 水
Yakeato / ni / sukitōri-keri / kan-no / mizu
Fire-ravaged-area / in / is-transparent-keri / midwinter's / water

Lightning flashes
where my wife has come from,
whither I go.

                              A red cricket.
                              My fever, glimmering,
                              reaches a peak.

稲 妻 す 妻 の 来 し 方 我 行 く 方
Inazuma / su / tsuma-no / koshi / kata / waga / yuku / kata
Lightning | makes | wife's | has-come | direction | my | going | direction

---

蟋 赤 し ほ の ぼ の 熱 の 上 る と き
Kōrogi / akashi / honobono / netsu-no / agaru / toki
Cricket | is-red | dimly | fever's | rises | when

Chestnut blossoms were fragrant
before I vomited blood—
and they are still.

                              As the drug takes hold,
                              the moon of the thirteenth night
                              scampers away from me.

栗 咲 く 香 血 を 喀 く 前 も そ の 後 も
Kuri / saku / ka / chi / o / haku / mae / mo / sono / ato / mo
Chestnut | blooming | fragrance | blood | (acc.) | vomit | before | also | that | after | also

---

麻 薬 う て ば 十 三 夜 月 遁 走 す
Mayaku / uteba / jūsanya-zuki / tonsō-su
Drug | when-inject | thirteenth-night-moon | runs-away
The ailing poet had to have four ribs removed in October 1948. Mayaku *refers to the anaesthetic used for the operation.*

Spring storm—
a corpse courageously
leaves the hospital.

So languidly
snowflakes fall, offering no
consolation to me.

春 嵐 屍 は 敢 え て 出 で ゆ く も
Haru / arashi / kabane / wa / aete / ide-yuku / mo
Spring / storm / corpse / as-for / courageously / goes-out / !

力 な く 降 る 雪 な れ ば な ぐ さ ま ず
Chikara / naku / furu / yuki / nareba / nagusamazu
Strength / non-existent / falling / snow / as-is / am-not-consoled

---

It snows quietly,
abundantly, and fast —
a mortuary.

On the way towards
the fountain I lag behind,
and how calm I feel!

雪 は し づ か に ゆ た か に は や し 屍 室
Yuki / wa / shizukani / yutakani / hayashi / kabaneshitsu
Snow / as-for / quietly / abundantly / is-fast / mortuary

泉 へ の 道 後 れ ゆ く 安 け さ よ
Izumi / e-no / michi / okure / yuku / yasukesa / yo
Fountain / to / road / lagging / go / calm / !

Hundreds and thousands
of earthen pipes, with their mouths
open, the snow falls.

With something in my heart
that will not stand up, I help
the bush clover to stand up.

百 千 の 土 管 口 あけ 雪 降 れ り
Hyaku / sen-no / dokan / kuchi / ake / yuki / fureri
Hundreds | thousands' | earthen-pipes | mouths | open | snow | falls

---

起 ち 上 ら ざ る も の 胸 に 萩 起 す
Tachiagarazaru / mono / mune / ni / hagi / okosu
Not-rising | thing | chest | in | bush-clover | raise

加 藤 楸 邨

Shūson was born in Tokyo on 26 May 1905. As a child he lived in many different places, because his father, a railway employee, was periodically transferred. His parents were Christians, and he too was baptized in 1920. Upon graduation from middle school he became a schoolteacher to help with the family finances. His thirst for better education was not to be quenched, however, and in 1937 he entered Tokyo College of Arts and Science, though he was already over thirty and had three children. Three years later he received a B LITT degree in Japanese literature and began teaching at a secondary school in Tokyo. He was an established haiku poet by this time, and in 1940 he founded his own magazine called *Thunder in Midwinter*. In 1944 he visited Korea, Mongolia, and China. The following year his house was destroyed in an air raid. In the gruelling years that followed the war his health began to fail, and he spent most of his time from 1948 to 1950 struggling to recover from pleurisy. He was restored to health again in 1952, and two years later he was appointed Professor of Japanese at Aoyama Gakuin Junior College in Tokyo, a post he still holds today. So far he has published ten collections of haiku, including *Thunder in Midwinter* (1939), *Sky after the Snow* (1943), *Memory of the Flames* (1948), *Mountain Range* (1955), and *Visionary Deer* (1968). He is also a highly respected Bashō scholar.

*I grieve, and there comes
a shrike, with golden sunbeams
on its back.*

*All that withers
has withered away, and the grove
reposes in calm.*

かなしめば鵙金色の日を負ひ来
Kanashimeba / mozu / konjiki-no / hi / o / oi / ku
When-grieve | shrike | gold-colour's | sun | (acc.) | bearing | comes

---

枯るるもの枯れゆき林しづかなり
Karuru / mono / kare-yuki / hayashi / shizukanari
Withering | things | withering-away | grove | is-quiet

Trees are in a haze —
something gleaming in the distance
has become a heron.

The winter tree
I am leaning on has turned
into a tank's roar.

木 木 霞 み 遠 ひ か る も の 鷺 と な り ぬ
Kigi / kasumi / tō-hikaru / mono / sagi / to / narinu
Trees | being-hazy | distantly-gleaming | thing | heron | to | has-turned

わ が 凭 り し 冬 木 戦 車 の 音 と な る
Waga / yorishi / fuyuki / sensha-no / oto / to / naru
My | leaning | winter-tree | tank's | sound | to | turns

I walk down a slope;
at the cold sunset glow
I shake my fist.

I kill an ant
and realize my three children
have been watching.

坂 く だ る 寒 き 夕 焼 に 腕 を 振 り
Saka / kudaru / samuki / yūyake / ni / ude / o / furi
Slope / descend / cold / evening-glow / in / arm / (acc.) / shaking

蟻 殺 す わ れ を 三 人 の 子 に 見 ら れ ぬ
Ari / korosu / ware / o / sannin-no / ko / ni / mirarenu
Ant / killing / I / (acc.) / three / children / by / have-been-seen

*From atop the roof
I gaze at the morning glow
that does not last long.*

*At a mantis
I brandish my hand—like
a mantis.*

屋 上 に 見 し 朝 焼 の な が か ら ず
Okujō / ni / mishi / asayake-no / nagakarazu
Rooftop | on | see | morning-glow's | is-not-long

蟷 螂 に 蟷 螂 の ご と く わ が 手 を 立 つ
Tōrō / ni / tōrō / no-gotoku / waga / te / o / tatsu
Mantis | at | mantis | like | my | hand | (acc.) | raise

I put out the light.
In my heart a precipice
before the moon.

On the scorching sand
lies a lost life, with its shape
impeccably preserved.

火 を 消 す や 心 崖 な す 月 の 前
Hi / o / kesu / ya / kokoro / gake / nasu / tsuki-no / mae
Light | (acc.) | put-out | : | heart | cliff | makes | moon's | before

---

灼 け 砂 に 果 て に し も の の 形 た だ し
Yakezuna / ni / hatenishi / mono-no / katachi / tadashi
Scorching-sand | on | perished | thing's | shape | is-perfect
Written in 1944, during the poet's travels to the Gobi Desert.

A pheasant, with eyes
defiantly glaring,
is being sold.

From the hydrangea's
shade a pair of eyes watch:
as I look, nothing.

雉子 の 眸 の か う か う と し て 売 ら れ け り
Kiji-no / me-no / kō-kō / to / shite / urare-keri
Pheasant's | eyes' | glare-glare | thus | doing | is-sold-keri
Written in late 1945, amid the social and moral upheavals caused by Japan's defeat in World War II. Some made easy
money in the black market, while honest men were starving.

紫 陽 花 の 蔭 に 目 が あ り 見 れ ば な し
Ajisai-no / kage / ni / me / ga / ari / mireba / nashi
Hydrangea's | shade | in | eyes | (nomin.) | there-are | when-look | are-non-existent

Thunder in midwinter:
the eyes of a dead friend
looking on, I live.

She was born a cat
and I was born a man—
we walk in the dew.

寒 雷 や 今 は 亡 き 目 を 負 ひ て 生 く
Kanrai / ya / ima / wa / naki / me / o / oite / iku
Midwinter-thunder / : / now / as-for / dead / eyes / (acc.) / bearing / live

猫 と 生 れ 人 間 と 生 れ 露 に 歩 す
Neko / to / umare / ningen / to / umare / tsuyu / ni / hosu
Cat / thus / being-born / man / thus / being-born / dew / in / walk

This frosty night a baby
cries, craving for something
far more than its parents.

Amid the snow
lies the corpse of a crow
with its eyes open.

霜 夜 子 は 泣 く 父 母 よ り は る か な る も の を 呼 び
Shimoyo / ko / wa / naku / fubo / yori / harukanaru / mono / o / yobi
Frosty-night / child / as-for / cries / parents / more-than / far-away / thing / (acc.) / calling

雪 の 中 鴉 の む く ろ 目 を あ け ゐ る
Yuki-no / naka / karasu-no / mukuro / me / o / ake / iru
Snow's / inside / raven's / corpse / eyes / (acc.) / open / is

Passing by, I see
an autumnal wind blowing
at a pine tree's wound.

A falling leaf:
the moment it reaches the ground
time slows down.

見 つ つ 過 ぐ 秋 風 が 松 の 傷 吹 く を
Mitsutsu / sugu / akikaze / ga / matsu-no / kizu / fuku / o
While-looking | pass | autumn-wind | (nomin.) | pine-tree's | wound | blows | (acc.)

落 葉 地 に と ど く や 時 間 ゆ る み け り
Ochiba / chi / ni / todoku / ya / jikan / yurumi-keri
Falling-leaf | ground | on | touches | that-instant | time | slackens-keri

The wind of autumn—
a chicken gazes at something
I cannot see.

The scent of citron
as I open my eyes to death
right beside me.

秋 の 風 鶏 の 見 る も の 我 に 見 え ぬ
Aki-no / kaze / tori-no / miru / mono / ware / ni / mienu
Autumn's / wind / chicken's / seeing / thing / me / by / is-not-seen

柚 子 匂 ふ す ぐ そ こ の 死 に 目 ひ ら け ば
Yuzu / niou / sugu / soko-no / shi / ni / me / hirakeba
Citron / smells / immediately / that-place's / death / at / eyes / when-open
Written in 1962, when the author, who was hospitalized from November 1960 to March 1962 because of a respiratory
illness, went through a series of operations.

西 東 三 鬼

Sanki was born on 15 May 1900, in an old castle town in the hilly region of western Honshu, where his father was a superintendent of county schools. Young Sanki first wanted to become an artist, but upon the advice of his elders he entered Nippon Dental College in Tokyo. Shortly after completing his training there, he went to Singapore to operate a dental clinic. His life there was by and large a happy one, but he was forced to return to Japan in 1929 when the political situation in the area grew tense. He started to practise dentistry in Tokyo, and it was then that he became interested in haiku. He quickly distinguished himself as a haiku poet, but his liberal attitude on current issues was viewed with suspicion by the ultra-nationalistic government of the day, and he was imprisoned for several months in 1940. Frustrated, he moved to Kobe and stopped writing haiku for a while. But when the war ended he resumed his literary activities with fervour. He helped set up several new haiku magazines, established the Modern Haiku Association, and became the editor of an influential monthly called *Haiku* for a time. During his relatively short career as a poet he published four collections of haiku: *Flag* (1940), *Night Peaches* (1948), *Today* (1951), and *Transfiguration* (1962). He died on 1 April 1962.

In the right eye,
an immense river: in the left
eye, a horseman.

Over arithmetic
a youngster voicelessly
weeps — summer.

右 の 眼 に 大 河 左 の 眼 に 騎 兵
Migi-no / me / ni / taiga / hidari-no / me / ni / kihei
Right | eye | in | large-river | left | eye | in | horseman

算 術 の 少 年 し の び な け り 夏
Sanjutsu-no / shōnen / shinobi-nakeri / natsu
Arithmetic's | youth | silently-weeps | summer

A machine gun—
in the middle of the forehead
red blossoms bloom.

A rooster:
beneath the fallen leaves
there is not a thing.

機 関 銃 眉 間 に 赤 き 花 が 咲 く
Kikanjū / miken / ni / akaki / hana / ga / saku
Machine-gun | between-eyebrows | in | red | blossoms | (nomin.) | bloom

雄 鶏 や 落 葉 の 下 に 何 も な き
Ondori / ya / ochiba-no / shita / ni / nani / mo / naki
Rooster | : | fallen-leaves' | underneath | in | anything | even | non-existent

Lying collapsed,
a scarecrow, and high above
its face, the heaven.

The endlessly
falling snow—I wonder what
it is bringing to me.

倒 れ た る 案 山 子 の 顔 の 上 に 天
Taore–taru / kakashi-no / kao / no-ue-ni / ten
Has-fallen / scarecrow's / face / above / heaven

限 り な く 降 る 雪 何 を も た ら す や
Kagirinaku / furu / yuki / nani / o / motarasu / ya
Limitlessly / falling / snow / what / (acc.) / brings / ?

Christmas Day —
there stands a stable, and
a horse is in it.

After eating whalemeat
orphans and a doctor start
a baseball game.

クリスマス馬小屋ありて馬が住む
Kurisumasu / uma-goya / arite / uma / ga / sumu
Christmas | horse-pen | there-is | horse | (nomin.) | lives

鯨食つて始まる孤児と医師の野球
Kujira / kutte / hajimaru / koji / to / ishi-no / yakyū
Whale | eating | begins | orphans | and | doctor's | baseball
A scene in postwar Japan, where there was a severe shortage of food and people often had to eat whalemeat. Undoubtedly
the orphans in the poem are children who lost parents in the war. They play baseball, one of the many American imports
that flooded postwar Japan.

The laughter lasts
forever in the distance
on the withered moor.

A patient rises
and wipes the window pane
soiled by winter.

いつまでも笑ふ枯野の遠くにて
Itsumademo / warau / kareno-no / tōku / nite
Forever | laughs | withered-moor's | distance | at

病者起ち冬が汚せる硝子拭く
Byōsha / tachi / fuyu / ga / yogoseru / garasu / fuku
Sick-person | rising | winter | (nomin.) | soiled | glass | wipes

On the ground of May
the dog ever increasingly
smells of dog.

On the other shore,
a person; the cold wind
connects me to him.

五 月 の 地 面 犬 は い よ い よ 犬 臭 く
Gogatsu-no / jimen / inu / wa / iyo-iyo / inu / kusaku
May's | ground | dog | as-for | more-more | dog | smelling

対 岸 の 人 と 寒 風 も て つ な が る
Taigan-no / hito / to / kanpū / mote / tsunagaru
Opposite-shore's | person | with | cold-wind | with | am-linked

---

The stonemason is young,
scattering fragments of stone
like blooms of autumn.

The raven has flown
away: flapping his wings
on the moor, a man.

石 工 若 し 散 る 石 片 が 秋 の 花
Ishiku / wakashi / chiru / sekihen / ga / aki-no / hana
Stonemason | is-young | scattering | stone-fragments | (nomin.) | autumn's | blossoms

---

鴉 飛 び 立 て り 羽 ば た く 枯 野 男
Karasu / tobi / tateri / habataku / kareno / otoko
Raven | flying | has-left | flapping | withered-moor | man

On the window pane
in front of an ailing face
snowflakes have stuck.

I sow sunflower seeds
and look up above the clouds
to locate the sun.

病 む 顔 の 前 の 硝 子 に 雪 張 り つ く
Yamu / kao-no / mae-no / garasu / ni / yuki / haritsuku
Ailing / face's / front's / glass / on / snow / sticks

向 日 葵 播 き 雲 の 上 な る 日 を 探 す
Himawari / maki / kumo / no-ue / naru / hi / o / sagasu
Sunflowers / sowing / clouds / above / is / sun / (acc.) / seek

Could I store it
in myself: a mountainful
of cicadas' screech!

Concentrating the strength
of the abandoned garden,
a sunflower stands.

身 に 貯 へ ん 全 山 の 蟬 の 声
Mi / ni / takuwaen / zenzan-no / semi-no / koe
Body / in / wish-to-store / whole-mountain's / cicadas' / voice

荒 園 の 力 あ つ ま り 向 日 葵 立 つ
Kōen-no / chikara / atsumari / himawari / tatsu
Deserted-garden's / strength / gathering / sunflower / stands

Autumn nightfall—
the skeleton of a huge fish
is drawn out to the sea.

The ocean would soak
my feet, if the crescent moon
hanged me by the neck.

秋 の 暮 大 魚 の 骨 を 海 が 引 く
Aki-no / kure / taigyo-no / hone / o / umi / ga / hiku
Autumn's / evening / large-fish's / bones / (acc.) / sea / (nomin.) / draws

海 に 足 浸 る 三 日 月 に 首 吊 ら ば
Umi / ni / ashi / hitaru / mikazuki / ni / kubi / tsuraba
Sea / in / feet / soak / crescent-moon / by / neck / if-hang

富 沢 赤 黄 男

Kakio was born on 14 July 1902 in a port city on the western coast of Shikoku. After finishing middle school in his home town he went to Tokyo and studied economics at Waseda University. Upon graduation in 1926 he joined a shipping firm, but was conscripted a few months later. In the army he belonged to the engineer corps and eventually attained the rank of lieutenant. In 1937 he was sent to China and took part in various battles for the next three years. In 1940 he was able to return to Japan, but a few months later he was again called back to active duty.

He spent the remainder of the war years with a force which was defending some small islands on the northern front. In the postwar period his creative energy spurted out. With Sōjō and several other poets he started a radical haiku magazine called *The Solar System* in 1946. In 1948 he created a magazine entitled *Palace of Poems* which published both haiku and non-haiku poems (a daring anti-traditionalist undertaking), and in 1952 he began another magazine, *Roses*, with a group of surrealist haiku poets. From about 1958 on, however, he seldom wrote poetry. He died on 7 March 1962. His haiku are collected in three books: *Wolf in Heaven* (1941), *Snake's Flute* (1952), and *Revelations* (1961).

Withered reeds—
I stuff them into my eyes
and trudge towards home.

As a butterfly
plummets, a thunderous crash
in the freezing season.

枯葦を瞳につめこんでたちもどる
Kareashi / o / me / ni / tsumekonde / tachimodoru
Withered-reeds | (acc.) | eyes | in | stuffing | return

蝶墜ちて大音響の結氷期
Chō / ochite / daionkyō-no / keppyō-ki
Butterfly | falling | large-sound's | freezing-season

A wandering horse,
turning into a longing
for home, vanishes.

Under the winter sky
it looks like a peony:
the woman's tongue.

彷徨へる馬郷愁となりて消ぬ
Samayoeru / uma / kyōshū / to / narite / kienu
Wandering | horse | nostalgia | to | turning | vanishes
Written when the author was serving in the army in central China.

冬天に牡丹のやうなひとの舌
Tōten / ni / botan / no-yōna / hito-no / shita
Winter-sky | in | peony's | like | person's | tongue

Camellias fall.
Ah, what a lukewarm
fire in the daytime!

The leopard's cage:
not a drop of water
in heaven.

椿 散 る あ あ な ま ぬ る き 昼 の 火 事
Tsubaki / chiru / aa / namanuruki / hiru-no / kaji
Camellias | fall | Ah | lukewarm | daytime's | fire
Written in the spring of 1940. The poet, discharged by the army, had just returned home from the battlefield overseas.

豹 の 檻 一 滴 の 水 天 に な し
Hyō-no / ori / itteki-no / mizu / ten / ni / nashi
Leopard's | cage | one-drop-of | water | heaven | in | non-existent

The rocks are dark
and a melancholy oyster
faintly gleams.

The autumnal wind
surpasses an empty snakeskin
in whiteness.

岩 黝 く 憂 愁 の 牡 蠣 う す び か る
Iwa / kuroku / yūshū-no / kaki / usubikaru
Rocks | being-dark | melancholy's | oyster | faintly-gleams
Entitled 'Frantic Scream.'

秋 風 は 蛇 の ぬ け が ら よ り 白 し
Akikaze / wa / hebi-no / nukegara / yori / shiroshi
Autumn-wind | as-for | snake's | empty-shell | more-than | is-white

---

As I cough
heaven above the leafless trees
coughs too.

In the sweltering sky
the sound of footsteps fades
and the laughter remains.

咳 け ば 枯 木 の 天 も 咳 け り
Shiwabukeba / kareki-no / ten / mo / shiwabukeri
When-cough | bare-trees' | heaven | also | coughs

炎 天 に 跫 音 き え て 哄 笑 は の こ る
Enten / ni / ashioto / kiete / kōshō / wa / nokoru
Flaming-sky | in | footsteps | vanishing | laughter | as-for | remains

Uttering a lie
with beautiful colours,
an icicle.

In the evening dusk
a mourning badge: a black dog
crouches.

嘘 吐 い て 光 彩 う つ く し き つ ら ら か な
Uso / tsuite / iro / utsukushiki / tsurara / kana
Lie / uttering / colours / beautiful / icicle / kana

黄 昏 の 喪 章 黒 犬 が う づ く ま る
Tasogare-no / moshō / kuroinu / ga / uzukumaru
Dusk's / mourning-badge / black-dog / (nomin.) / crouches
The moshō, *made of black silk and shaped like a butterfly, is attached to the mourner's clothes at a funeral.*

Grapes, each one of them with resilience, and clouds.

Man's wisdom flickers, flickers— a light trap.

葡 萄 一 粒 一 粒 の 弾 力 と 雲
Budō / hitotsubu / hitotsubu-no / danryoku / to / kumo
Grapes | one-berry | one-berry's | resilience | and | clouds

人 間 の 智 慧 ゆ ら ゆ ら と 誘 蛾 燈
Ningen-no / chie / yura-yura / to / yūgatō
Man's | wisdom | flicker-flicker | thus | light-trap
Yūgatō is an oil lamp to which a shallow receptacle filled with oil is attached. Noxious insects, attracted to the light, come and fall into the oil.

I keep rubbing an awl,
in the darkness of despair
I keep rubbing an awl.

Brightness that lies
in the clouds: darkness
that lies in the reeds.

錐 を も む 暗 澹 と し て 錐 を も む
Kiri / o / momu / antan / to / shite / kiri / o / momu
Awl / (acc.) / rub / dark-gloom / thus / doing / awl / (acc.) / rub
Kiri is a pointed instrument used for boring a hole. The user rubs it between his hands, much in the same way the primitives rubbed a stick to start fire. The gesture somewhat resembles that of a man praying with his hands together.

雲 に あ る あ か る さ 葦 に あ る く ら さ
Kumo / ni / aru / akarusa / ashi / ni / aru / kurasa
Clouds / in / there-is / brightness / reeds / in / there-is / darkness

---

Within her eyes
ant, ant, ant, ant, ant.

Spring:
white eggs
and white eggs' shadows.

ひとの瞳の中の蟻蟻蟻蟻蟻
Hito-no / me / no-naka-no / ari / ari / ari / ari / ari
Person's / eyes / in / ant / ant / ant / ant / ant

春 は 白 い 卵 と 白 い 卵 の 影 と
Haru / wa / shiroi / tamago / to / shiroi / tamago-no / kage / to
Spring / as-for / white / eggs / and / white / eggs' / shadows / and

---

Good will?
How far do the rings
of zeros extend?

Like a conclusion
it crouches on the ground—
a toad.

善 意 ? ど こ ま で つ づ く 零 の 環 よ
Zen'i / ? / doko / made / tsuzuku / zero-no / wa / yo
Goodwill | ? | where | to | continue | zero's | rings | !

結 論 の ご と く 地 に 跼 し 蟇
Ketsuron / no-gotoku / chi / ni / kyoshi / hikigaeru
Conclusion | like | ground | on | crouching | toad

Tōta was born on 23 September 1919 in a town northwest of Tokyo where, aside from a two years' stay in Shanghai, he spent most of his boyhood. He then studied economics at Tokyo University, graduating in 1943. He immediately began working for the Bank of Japan, but a few months later had to go into the army. He was in the vicinity of the Truk Islands for most of his service days. He returned to Japan after the end of the war and resumed his work as a bank employee. He was transferred successively to branch offices in Fukushima, Kobe, and Nagasaki. He had started to write haiku as a young boy under the influence of his father, who was a regular contributor to *Staggerbush*. Tōta's taste, however, was more for the 'humanist' haiku, and he chose to send his work to *Thunder in Midwinter*. He is still close to Shūson's group today, though he is affiliated with other haiku groups as well. He has published four volumes of haiku so far, the latest being *Topography of the Dark Green Land* (1972). He has also written a great deal on the art of haiku, including two books entitled *Today's Haiku* (1965) and *Haiku* (1972). He works now at the headquarters of the Bank of Japan in Tokyo.

A slug
bathed in an ethereal glow
near a chicken.

High school boys
are talking of God, while the snow
keeps piling up on the ricks.

なめくじり寂光を負ひ鶏のそば
Namekujiri / jakkō / o / oi / tori-no / soba
Slug | ethereal-glow | (acc.) | carrying | chicken's | proximity

---

中学生神語りおり雪積む藁
Chūgakusei / kami / katari / ori / yuki / tsumu / wara
Secondary-school-students | God | talking | are | snow | piles | straw

---

Dead bones
must be dumped into the sea!
I chew a piece of takuan.

The graveyard is burnt too:
cicadas, like pieces of flesh,
on the trees.

死 に し 骨 は 海 に 捨 つ べ し 沢 庵 嚙 む
Shinishi / hone / wa / umi / ni / sutsu / beshi / takuan / kamu
Dead | bones | as-for | sea | in | dump | must | takuan *| chew*
Takuan, *pickled radish, was one of the last food items an average Japanese could get during the war years.*

墓 地 も 焼 跡 蟬 肉 片 の ご と 樹 々 に
Bochi / mo / yakeato / semi / nikuhen / no-goto / kigi / ni
Graveyard | also | fire-site | cicadas | flesh-pieces | like | trees | on
Written in the Hongō district of Tokyo, an area that suffered heavy air raids during World War II.

Above the crumbled bricks
a butterfly, its heart attached
here to the slums.

On the hill, a withered farm;
in the valley, no cogitation.
Clear water is all.

崩 れ 煉 瓦 に 蝶 執 着 す こ こ ス ラ ム
Kuzure / renga / ni / chō / shūjaku-su / koko / suramu
Crumbled | bricks | on | butterfly | feels-attachment | here | slums

山 に は 枯 畑 谷 に は 思 惟 な く た だ 澄 む 水
Yama / ni / wa / karehata / tani / ni / wa / shii / naku / tada / sumu / mizu
Hill | on | as-for | withered-farm | valley | in | as-for | cogitation | non-existent | only | clear | water

'*A slave's freedom*'—*so says
the phrase: an egg in midwinter
serene on the plate.*

*Like something totally
alien, a fresh pine cone
sits upright on the grass.*

奴 隷 の 自 由 と い う 語 寒 卵 皿 に 澄 み
Dorei-no / jiyū / to / yū / go / kantamago / sara / ni / sumi
Slave's | freedom | thus | says | word | midwinter-egg | plate | on | being-serene

異 質 の ご と 新 し き 松 か さ 草 に 正 坐
Ishitsu / no-goto / atarashiki / matsukasa / kusa / ni / seiza
Heterogeneity | like | new | pine-cone | grass | on | sits-upright

Ephemerae swarming
at a bridge lamp—I arrive
and gain a shadow.

At many street corners
streetwalkers fight with each other—
tangerines are dry.

蜉蝣むらがる橋燈に来て影を得る
Kagerō / muragaru / kyōtō / ni / kite / kage / o / uru
Ephemerae | swarming | bridge-lamp | at | coming | shadow | (acc.) | gain

---

あまたの街角街娼争い蜜柑乾く
Amata-no / machikado / gaishō / arasoi / mikan / kawaku
Many | street-corners | streetwalkers | fighting | tangerines | dry

*It joins a group—
a killifish, swiftly
and happily.*

*Is it afraid
of peace? Coal in summertime
covered with straw mats.*

群 に 入 る 目 高 素 早 く 幸 福 に
Mure / ni / iru / medaka / subayaku / kōfuku-ni
Group / into / enters / killifish / swiftly / happily

平 和 お そ れ る や 夏 の 石 炭 蓆 か ぶ り
Heiwa / osoreru / ya / natsu-no / sekitan / mushiro / kaburi
Peace / fears / ? / summer's / coal / straw-mats / being-covered
Written during the Korean War.

Factory dismissing the workers—
it vomits cloudy autumn water
into the canal.

A white human figure
far, far away, walks on the farm
in order not to fade.

首切る工場秋曇の水を運河に吐き
Kubi / kiru / kōba / shūdon-no / mizu / o / unga / ni / haki
Heads / cutting / factory / autumn-cloudiness's / water / (acc.) / canal / into / vomiting
Written in Amagasaki, an industrial city near Osaka. Kubi (o) kiru *is an idiom meaning 'to dismiss (from employment).'*

白い人影はるばる田をゆく消えぬために
Shiroi / hitokage / haru-baru / ta / o / yuku / kienu / tame / ni
White / human-figure / far-far / farm / (acc.) / go / not-fade / effort / in

---

Under the girders of the bridge
vomit is stuck, blooming
as winter's blossoms.

After a heated argument
I go out to the street
and become a motorcycle.

ガ ー ド 下 に は り つ く 反 吐 が 冬 の 華
Gādo / shita / ni / haritsuku / hedo / ga / fuyu-no / hana
Girder | underneath | in | sticks | vomit | (nomin.) | winter's | blossom

激 論 つ く し 街 ゆ き オ ー ト バ イ と 化 す
Gekiron / tsukushi / machi / yuki / ōtobai / to / kasu
Heated-argument | ending | street | going | auto-bike | to | change

Like an arm overstretched
and tired, reddish brown smoke
rising from a steel mill.

                                        Like squids
                                        bank clerks are fluorescent
                                        from the morning.

手が長くだるし赤茶けた製鋼煙
Te / ga / nagaku / darushi / akachaketa / seikōen
Hand | (nomin.) | long | is-tired | reddish-brown | steelmaking-smoke

---

銀行員等朝より螢光す烏賊のごとく
Ginkōin-ra / asa / yori / keikō / su / ika / no-gotoku
Bank-clerks | morning | from | fluorescence | make | squids | like

Every one of the mouths
is beautiful—late in summer
a jazz group.

Strong are the youngsters
even on a day when onions
rot at the dry beach.

どれも口美し晩夏のジャズ一団
Dore / mo / kuchi / utsukushi / banka-no / jazu / ichidan
Any / also / mouth / is-beautiful / late-summer's / jazz / one-group

---

強し青年干潟に玉葱腐る日も
Tsuyoshi / seinen / higata / ni / tamanegi / kusaru / hi / mo
Are-strong / youths / dry-beach / on / onions / rot / day / even

---

e	*Indicates direction: 'in the direction of, ' 'to.'*
ga	*Conjunction suggesting incongruity: 'on the contrary,' 'but.' The incongruity may be very slight or ambiguous.*
-ga (1)	*Nominative particle; indicates the subject of a sentence or clause.*
-ga (2)	*Particle joining two nouns, where the preceding noun modifies or limits the meaning of the noun that follows. Used primarily in literary Japanese.*
ka	*Interrogative particle; can be considered a question mark pronounced.*
kamo	*Same as kana, but slightly more archaic and masculine in its emotive effect.*
kana	*Emphasizes the speaker's emotion without specifying it. Thus a poet who dislikes particularizing his emotion often chooses to end his poem with* kana, *leaving out his main verb.*
-keri	*Terminal particle; adds more emotion to the preceding verb when used in poetry.*
koso	*Strongly emphasizes the preceding word or words; more emphatic than* zo.
made	*Indicates the terminal point of a continuing action: 'up to," 'as far as.'*
mo	*'Also' or 'even.' In rare cases it is used as an equivalent of* kamo.
ni (1)	*Indicates general location: 'in,' 'on,' 'at,' 'into,' etc.*
ni (2)	*Indicates the purpose or object of an action: 'for the sake of,' 'in order to,' 'to.'*
ni (3)	*Indicates the agent in a passive or causative expression: 'by.'*
-no	*Same as -ga (2), but more colloquial and far more commonly used today.*
o	*Accusative particle; indicates the direct object of the verb to follow.*
-tari	*Indicates the presence of the result(s) of an action just completed, or confirms the continuation into the present of an action initiated in the past.*
to (1)	*Joins two nouns on a plane of parity: 'and,' 'as well as,' 'together with.' When obvious, one of the nouns may be omitted.*
to (2)	*Conjunction indicating time: 'whereupon,' 'then.'*
to (3)	*Particle marking the end of a quotation or quotation-like word or words: 'thus (he spoke, thought, etc.).'*
wa	*Indicates the topic of a sentence: 'as for.'*
ya (1)	*Emphasizes the preceding word or words. In haiku it is often used as the so-called 'cutting-word,' dividing the poem into two parts and inviting the reader to discover their interrelationship by himself. It is somewhat like a colon in English punctuation, since there is usually an implied equation between the two parts thus separated.*
ya (2)	*Same as ka, but used only in literary Japanese.*
yo (1)	*Makes the preceding verb imperative.*
yo (2)	*Adds more emotion to the preceding word or words. Used in colloquial Japanese also, while* kana *is strictly literary.*
zo	*Confirms emphatically the meaning of the preceding word or words; slightly less emphatic than* koso.